The Sol Plaatje European Union
Poetry Anthology 2011

The Sol Plaatje European Union Poetry Anthology 2011

Compiled by Liesl Jobson

First published by Jacana Media (Pty) Ltd in 2011

10 Orange Street
Sunnyside
Auckland Park 2092
South Africa
+2711 628 3200
www.jacana.co.za

© Individual authors, 2011

All rights reserved.

ISBN 978-1-4314-0275-5
Job No. 001609

Cover design Shawn Paikin and Maggie Davey
Set in Ehrhardt 11/13pt
Printed by Ultra Litho (Pty) Limited, Johannesburg

See a complete list of Jacana titles at www.jacana.co.za

Contents

Foreword *Liesl Jobson* ix

It is a risk *Ingrid Andersen* 1
Sterkfontein Bones *Christine M Coates*. 2
Remembering Afghanistan *Christine M Coates* 4
Anatomy *Gail Dendy* 5
With her Feet on the Ground *Gail Dendy* 7
Don't Speak *Gail Dendy*. 8
The Anatomy of Poetry *Dawn Garisch*. 11
Miracle *Dawn Garisch*. 12
Digger *Dawn Garisch* 14
Sitting *Anthea Garman*. 17
For Gemma *Anthea Garman* 18
A Terrible Beauty *Denise Gray* 19
In the Balance *Dorian Haarhoff* 20
Curry Kindling *Dorian Haarhoff*. 21
Weather and Season Song *Dorian Haarhoff* 22
Chernobyl *Megan Hall*. 24
Blushing brides *Megan Hall* 27
my mentor is dressing me *Geoffrey Haresnape*. 28
My Ma se Blues *Siddiq Khan*. 31
Song *Siddiq Khan* 34
Prelude for Solo and Group Voices *Siddiq Khan* . . . 35
Ubomi *Nosipho Kota*. 36
Life *Nosipho Kota* 37

she imagines *Luisa Lagerwall*	38
the city *Luisa Lagerwall*	40
manning road *Luisa Lagerwall*	42
The uncomfortable silence *Jennifer Lovemore-Reed*	43
Ku Cindzuka ka Lwase *Risimati Mathonsi*	44
The Ripening of Lust *Risimati Mathonsi*	45
Ku Jayivha na N'wayingwani *Risimati Mathonsi*	46
Jive with N'wayingwani *Risimati Mathonsi*	48
Dithoto *Kea' Modimoeng*	50
Assets *Kea' Modimoeng*	52
Ba lebetse batlhoki *Kea' Modimoeng*	54
They have forgotten the poor *Kea' Modimoeng*	56
Phamokate wa ratha wa fenetha *Tsela Moloi*	58
The rage of Aids *Tsela Moloi*	61
Thabure *Tsela Moloi*	64
Thabure *Tsela Moloi*	66
For Your Drinking Pleasure *Jackie Mondi*	68
List of Sound Effects *Kobus Moolman*	69
Eight Critical Questions *Kobus Moolman*	71
His Explanation *Kobus Moolman*	72
Runaway *Dashen Naicker*	73
O a ipona *Puleng Nkomo*	74
He is full of himself *Puleng Nkomo*	75
Ga gešo mekgotheng *Puleng Nkomo*	76
In my neighbourhood *Puleng Nkomo*	78
Natla tša ntwa ya tokologo *Puleng Nkomo*	80

Heroes of war of freedom *Puleng Nkomo* 83
Soekers *Martha Pretoors* 85
Seekers *Martha Pretoors* 86
Verlore beeltenis *Martha Pretoors* 88
Lost Picture *Martha Pretoors* 89
After Battiss *Gillian Rennie* 90
I Remember Bethesda *Gillian Rennie* 91
Your Heart was a Squatter-Camp *Beverly Rycroft* . 93
Has your Dad got a bird yet? *Beverly Rycroft* 94
The wind at Uilenskraalmond *Karin Schimke* 97
Robben Island: Museum in the Making
  Mavis Smallberg 98
Remembering prisons and prisoners
  Abu Bakr Solomons 102
Lovuka lelosiko *Bhekani Thabede* 106
Tradition Awakens Again *Bhekani Thabede* 109
Trampled *Chris van der Walt* 112
For Maria Pilar *Chris van der Walt* 113
The last autumn leaf *Chris van der Walt* 115
Far Away *Tania van Schalkwyk* 116
Fathomless *Tania van Schalkwyk* 117
Matchstick Girl *Tania van Schalkwyk* 119

Biographies 121
What is the European Union? 133

Foreword

"It is a risk to open up words" greets the reader in the very first poem is this, the very first EU Sol Plaatje Poetry Award anthology. A perfect introduction for those who approach this alphabetically structured collection in a spirit of enquiry. What unfolds here? What is to be found in the astonishing range of voices represented between these covers? What hidden message lingers between the lines? And for all those who entered the contest, the questions: what was chosen, what found favour?

Committing to a poem is typically a mysterious process, whether submitting to the compulsion to write one or whether one engages in its reading. "It is a risk..." The poet's warning speaks to the wordsmith transfiguring the dross of daily life into the gold of conscious reflection. She addresses the reader who opens his or her being to the redemptive power of poetry's artistic observation. It is also an admonishment to the judge.

It is a risk to judge a poetry contest. All those plosives and vowels, shapeshifting before your eyes; the vibrant urgent narratives representing the soul of the country, all those phrases forging the contemporary myths, the stanzas that document the daily drama.

How to assess? How to find the best? Define *that* if you will, or divine it... Wherein lies the magic? Are these curses or spells? What a plethora of vital, vibrant voices presented themselves when the call went out for submissions. From first-timers to award-winning writers, the diversity of the 180 contributions (150 English, 30 indigenous languages) that arrived was most exciting. The poems received commented on the South African landscape and its politics, its sea shells and housing, its joggers and village girls, its illness and strength.

Epics and haikus, sonnets and free verse, poem after poem spoke to the state of the nation and the range of realities its people encounter. Poets who have written for years without formal recognition and some who have only just begun appear in this anthology beside poets whose names appear regularly in literary journals and at literary award ceremonies. However, the poems that arrived in the judges' mailboxes contained no names and were judged blind.

How to assess? Inspiring the process was the remarkable forefather of South African literature, pioneer of the imagination and namesake of this competition, Sol Plaatje. Kader Asmal once described him as one who had "the ability to weave between the different languages and cultures, and to contribute through writing, literature and journalism, to the betterment of the lives of South Africans."

Can poetry contribute to the betterment of South African life? Without doubt. The risk taking that is the poet's business improves us. As we reflect – via the poetic conscience performing its function – on the soft underbelly of every aspect of our humanity we are called to life and consciousness. Reconsidering our history and reflecting on the present through the aesthetic lens of the poet we stand a chance. Encountering the creative spirit in full integrity, there enters the possibility that we might be birthed into an awareness that prompts our evolution towards wisdom, compassion and integrity.

This was the guiding spirit behind judging this competition which was made possible by the generous sponsorship of the European Union. Making the first selection sought the works that struck an authentic note, showed attention to craft, that were unafraid and unashamed. These are poems that did not preach, that did not tell the reader how to think. This selection went to the next round. These are the poems representing the broad creative energy alive on every street in this country. These are the poems appearing in this anthology.

Vonani Bila (judging the indigenous languages), Robert Berold and Charl-Pierre Naudé (judging Afrikaans and English) drew up a short list that went to the final judge, the nation's poet laureate. Keorapetse Kgositsile sought in the winners those poems that thrust to the gut, cause the involuntary wince and spark the unanticipated gasp.

If ever we needed voices that speak with gritty but truthful tongues it is now. This anthology welcomes the sacred and profane reflections mirroring the banal and the beautiful of our loves and our landscape, our cities and psyche. Future anthologies of future competitions hope to absorb many more entries from South Africans of every walk of life. This is the call to poets of every persuasion to sharpen their skills, to study and practise. Above all it is an injunction to those with aspirations of being poets to read, read, read.

Can poetry contribute to the betterment of South African life? How can it not?

Liesl Jobson

It is a risk

To open up words,
unfold them to paper.

Found vowels,
hidden sibilants
chosen plosives

change shape
on a page.

INGRID ANDERSEN

Sterkfontein Bones

The cave holds the bones
the cave and also the hospital.
Sterkfontein, dust as old as stone.
She wondered if it had changed,
if there was concrete or
wooden walkways, a shop
that sold resin skulls for lamps.

The narrow opening still
concealed by kiepersol and wild olive,
she saw the bright bones –
a toe and a tooth.
It's called The Cradle now
but it's really a trapdoor –
animals fell in to die
on a heap of bones.

The other Sterkfontein
they called *Groendakkies*.
They took Papa there,
said he was mad;
bi-polar they call it today.
Hitler had it too,
a lithium pill can change history.

She sat with him on a bench there
under yellow apples of a syringa tree
What men don't understand, they
call madness,
she'd read it somewhere.
He wanted her to pick up the apples
that had fallen;
the silver apples of the moon
the golden apples of the sun,
but she would not.
Even if she did
she'd only have bones –
a tooth and a toe.

        CHRISTINE M COATES

Remembering Afghanistan

There is a prayer that changes the world
but I can't remember it.
I pick up five stones –
Kabul, Gaza, New York City, Somalia, Jerusalem.

God knows the grass is green here,
trees have a secret life.
Only those willing to climb to the top
will hear their whisper.
What do you think when people
are bombed all winter?

The sound of water is what I think.

The prayer of five stones –
Kabul, Gaza, New York City, Somalia, Jerusalem.
There is a prayer that changes the world.
I can't remember it.
The sound of water is what I think.

CHRISTINE M COATES

Anatomy

Between my shoulder blades
the slim rope of my spine
curves downwards
towards my hips.

If I lie with you
on your wide bed,
my spine
will be regarded
as smiling,

smiling when I am asleep,
and pursed-lipped
when I am awake,

and it is a birch tree
in the bare winter,
and a sapling
in the blue summer,

and it is the compass needle
of my days
and the bell-rope
of my nights,

and before I was born
it resembled a musical clef,
and afterwards
it will lie in the earth
as a broken string
of pearls,

and they say
pearls are for tears,
but if I were you,

and you my beloved,
I should not weep
for my spine,

for it is safe
between the arrowheads
of my shoulder blades,
pointing towards
the country
of my hips.

          GAIL DENDY

With her Feet on the Ground

My sister sat with her feet on the ground.
My sister pulled down birds from the sky.

She pulled them down with her tiny whistle,
with her tiny whistle through the gap in her teeth,

through the gap in her teeth she pulled them down,
pulled them to nest in her wild, grey hair,

in her wild, grey hair and her yellow skin,
her skin that was yellow as the desert sand,

the sand that was hard as my sister's feet,
her feet that were bare on the desert sand,

my sister pulled down birds from the sky,
she pulled them down with her tiny whistle,

through the gap in her teeth she drew them down,
and her feet, like two birds, escaped wild and free.

GAIL DENDY

Don't Speak

Don't speak to me of love:
the mouse will squeak
as though the rusty catch
of the old mousetrap
has slammed right down,
and all for a piece of cheese.
No, don't speak to me of love.

Don't speak to me of love:
the cattle are far too thin,
the goat's skin not yet
stretched enough
to make a worthy drum.
My ancestors squeal
in the night like whelps
and all that's said
can be nothing good.
No, don't speak to me of love.

Don't speak to me of love:
this thing with enough eyes
for a peacock-fan, this thing
as strong as a Masai man,
this thing as soft
as a newborn's bum.
No, don't speak to me of love.

Don't speak to me of love:
each word as polished
as a fine bright bead,
this thing of collars,
a harness, sinew,
this thing that drives
and harries you.
No, don't speak to me of love.

Don't speak to me of love:
I'll take no note,
put a guard on the door,
have an assegai ready in my hand.
I'll call out the shaman
with his evil eye.
No, don't speak to me of love.

Don't speak to me of love:
though the grain is good
and the crop grows high,
I won't listen at all,
I won't dignify your words
with my attention.
And I certainly won't reply.

Don't speak to me of love:
I say gather up your words,
don't scatter them.

Don't speak to me of love:
I shall be coming to you
very, very soon.

                GAIL DENDY

The Anatomy of Poetry

It seems my heart is not a pump;
nor gristly fist that's primed to clutch
and clench and thereby force
my life blood forward.

A thoughtful surgeon found this poem –
he unpicked the heart's impeccable stitch
along its seam, and found that it's
a twisted rope – double-twisted –
looped and helixed back upon itself.

He stopped to note the knotted heart's
faithful labour, and saw: it wrings blood out,
cup by careful cupful – more akin to washing
day, than to that of fitted factory parts.

The anatomy of poetry is often lost
within the eye's design. And at such cost.

DAWN GARISCH

Miracle

I wished for miracles when I was young
– like Thomas, who saw the stabbed
hands of Jesus, and slid his fingers
right inside His wounded heart.

There was the miracle of a man
who loved and wished to marry me;
yet, from another angle, this was
unremarkable. The inconceivable miracle

of our children – their lives arriving
out of mine – was also, strangely, ordinary.
The sacrament of marriage – which I had taken
to be flesh and blood – converted miraculously

back to paper, and, with surprising ease,
was lost. Then the nails, thorns, the long
strung stay; waiting for the ever-hopeful flesh
finally to surrender. A burial behind stone –

these things are commonplace. The year
of the third infidelity, third time denied,
my heart and sex stabbed, all that's sacred
butchered, knived – the last day of that year,

it was still, and cloudless. I needed a tempest
to rage and scourge the pain, debride my hurt,
and with rain to re-annoint me. I might, even,
have prayed. That night, unseasonably,

light cracked the sky's slate, and thunder rolled
the stone aside. Hot spats pattered; then water
drummed its fingers down upon the house.
I was re-made that night – composed

within the tender power of miracle.
Before the brave new year unsheathed its blade
in order to dispatch that which could no longer
serve, I went to urinate, and found that I had bled.

DAWN GARISCH

Digger

He digs a hole:
 I am of the earth, I understand its substance. In dreams I have a pebble in my mouth; a stone lies under my head. I know the way in: my muscles drive into the substratum; sunlight spills in to fill the gap. Again and again, stave and spill, widening the breach. The rhythm of labourers, the heart, of sex and drums. I could fit in there now, I could curl up in the dusty cup and let them bury me, the sods jarring my jelly flesh, soil sifting into cavities. That is how the wives of great men used to die, sealed into tombs with the sacred corpse, their breath stopped by the rising earth.
 Not my wife, she lives in modern times, and I fall far from great.

She does the washing up:
 My hands swim like fish among the dishes. I wash these plates daily, erasing the stains of ten thousand dinners, restoring whiteness and order. I rub and rub, the glaze wears thin and cracks appear, the clay crumbles and disintegrates between my fingers until the sink is full of a brown sediment.
 Through the kitchen window I see him bent over his excavations, busy with mud pies in the back garden. He has forgotten us; only when the children come home and run shouting and happy to see him does he raise his eyes and remember who he is.

The hole gets bigger:
The heat rolls off the great mountain of my body, washed away by stinging streams that flood the plains of my chest, the small of my back. I have found an old bone and pieces of china, objects that survive our broken lives. They are precious to me, reminding me of my finiteness, my fragility, the permanence of the earth. I shall keep them in a jar in the garage in a corner as I did when I was a child. I would mine for hours in the field next to our house looking for treasure. I found a brass catch, a marble, a broken chain and pieces of painted porcelain. My mother found them and threw them away. Few see the value of broken and discarded things.

My children are home, they tumble out of the back door and clamour around me. Their eyes are bright, like prospectors tracking their dreams. With their spades they pry open the soil. They are like two flints I keep discovering anew.

She waits:
Dinner gets cold on the table; I carry a stone in my chest. Every morning I make a promise: I will not argue with him today, I will not expose my need. Every day gravel collects in my mouth; the stone expands to fill my chest. If he looked he would notice how silt is filtering into the house. He would see how my legs are tired of carrying stones, of wading against the flow. He would notice that I am in danger of sinking.

At night I dream my bed is made of a thousand hands; a multitude of people carry me high and safe. Like the wind they carry me softly over rocky terrain; so high no dust storm can touch me, no mountain can bring me down.

He goes to bed:
She has turned off the light and lies in a dark room. I cannot tell whether she sleeps or waits. Even in sleep she wears a mantle I cannot penetrate, even as we make love I cannot touch her.

Tomorrow I will put the last rocks in place, the earth will settle, the cement will dry. We will plant ferns and lilies while water fills the pond, then my children will release the fish: golden ones and black.

I will ask her to come outside and look. When she sees she may smile; if I put my arm around her, perhaps she will laugh. Together we will stand and laugh while our children feed the fish.

DAWN GARISCH

Sitting

Sitting
still
watching the sculptor
who watches me
and then works on my head

watching my head
emerge
not like me

Unlike?
Or dislike?

I look at this
dull clay thing
that is supposed to be me
and think
how hard
how cold
how bony

It is skull
browbone
nose and chin

He seeks to be true to me
and my alarm
grows as he gets nearer
me

    ANTHEA GARMAN

For Gemma

When I wash
her little pink feet
they come clean

Mine I scrape,
scrub and scour
But the dirt is rooted
in the cracks and pores

I carry it all with me now

    ANTHEA GARMAN

A Terrible Beauty

I want to emerge from death
like you did, twice.

First from sterile sheets, bleep-beat box and
umbilical drip

to be less bruised,
homed in us, alighted.

Then from ground and body,
wheels to sky

that pen our new year's ageing lines.
We move to inhabit your resolutions.

I will pull your death around me;
softly cocooned, pending flight.

                                    DENISE GRAY

In the Balance

this woman with sticks,
looped in a ring of wire
bundled into one load,
steps out of the desert.
bearing wood for one burning.

this pile will flicker away
part of the night in the
dry quick burn. this snap
of desert kindling raised
on head and arms.

she moves as a man
on high wire, the pole
extending his arms
to hold the see-saw centre
sprung across his shoulders.

above the hushed ancestor crowd
who will her not to fall
off the dust-line into hunger,
she balances for a moment
her family in these branches.

              DORIAN HAARHOFF

Curry Kindling

alive in the dish
the colours spark
like glowing coals
and wood chips
aflame in the grate.

aromas drift past
banana and coconut
up the chimney
of my cheekbone,
sinus and nose.

red-green-yellow
and saffron flames
lick turmeric tongues,
warm masala mouths,
spice the throat,
funnel down into
the bowl of the belly.

the blaze crackles
in our onion stomachs,
simmers the breath,
blushes cheeks. embers
hiss, splutter, whoosh
into the Buddha laugh,
setting our hearts on fire.

DORIAN HAARHOFF

Weather and Season Song

in this Cape of Storms,
waves rear on hind legs
like polar bears
slashing the sky.
gale wind drives rain
parallel to the earth
through the vineyard,
splitting the oak,
flooding the Flats,
cracking the sea wall
like an egg shell.

sweating dog-summers
pant and howl in the face
of a fynbos fire
that chokes the air
and hurls pine cone
grenades at houses
and sears the mountain
coal-mine black.
sudden summer rain rots crops.

all seasons in a day –
nothing new, we say
to this western Cape.
yet where are
the in-between seasons,
when the earth tilts
with the sun shining
on Cancer or Capricorn?

somebody has flicked the
random scramble CD switch.
the weather and seasons,
out of sync, no longer
sing in four part harmony
the cycle song of creation –
spring summer autumn winter –
ordered and measured
in tones and moods
as in Vivaldi's Four Seasons.

and is that somebody us?

        DORIAN HAARHOFF

Chernobyl

900 years is long to wait
for the grass to grow clean again.

By then, Piotr and the other 400 souls
who could not bear to leave the dead zone

will long be dead: Piotr dead as he sits in his donkey cart
riding down roads that few now travel;

buried by someone slightly tougher,
in an overgrown garden, where the soil is hot;

soil that sucked in radiation, & held it
like a child sucking cooldrink through a straw.

◉

The cemetery is closed. No one can visit the dead
in this dead zone: the rubble someone buried there,

in true Soviet style, sets the whole graveyard ticking.
The dosimeter doesn't lie.

◉

The fishing magazines abandoned in the mailbox
are the least of it: Chernobyl birthed its survivors

naked into the world, having taken away the last treasures
– photos, letters – chosen as secret talismans,

before a chemical shower.
All must go, all could kill.

Littering the floor of an abandoned school:
drawings, dolls, small shoes. Surely the children cried

when they missed these? Or were their other losses
too great for these to matter? The only past they could take

was what they carried inside them as memory.
Passports, pictures of ancestors, certificates from school –

these people were detached from their verifiable history,
left wondering if they themselves really existed.

Ships in the harbour. Trains. Row upon row of army
trucks.
Fire engines, helicopters, personal cars, office equipment,

the contents of every shop in every street –
all were left behind, all were lost.

I try to imagine this happening here – not so unlikely
with Koeberg squatting on Cape Town's doorstep like a
toad.

I try to imagine the city lost, the harbour closed, every
ship left to rot,
every crane left to swing in the south-easter.

Every house and shack empty, every taxi left behind
as if in a wall-to-wall strike.

Leaving my own life, my home, the work of years, the
memories in objects.
Leaving with daughter and husband, nothing else.

No more vegetable garden at the Cape, two oceans
meeting, Castle,
or cable car moving like a fly up a string.

Cape Town chopped off, circumcised with bush school
savagery.

MEGAN HALL

Blushing brides

The pink heads of blushing brides,
the sharp hot mauve of waxy tea-tree blooms:
how strange that cut flowers on the way to their deaths
should make up for your missing handwriting on envelopes.

MEGAN HALL

my mentor is dressing me

he is a mature man
working with the skin of a tsessebe
for my loins
fitting me out with arrows and a tight-sewn quiver

in my hands a bow
taut taut bow ready for pulling

I pad with my feet on the floor
I bow forward at the waist
turning in a circle
looking into corners

what is it that I seek?
who am I hunting?
I want an item
a something
oh, I need a specific
and I will gain a specific

in these circumstances
I throw my learned procedures to the winds
to the seventy winds

language flows through me
like a stream
I am blustering with words

the folks in the circle
egg me on
it's a full room like a place for a party
but I cannot remain
to enjoy the samoosas and the designer water

I must be stalking
the moon is turning full
with the arrow's notch I will straddle the string

is it up that I must point?
do I point to the floor?
must I swing with the loaded shaft
to the door?
to the window?
to the facelessness of the wall?

the time is coming
to make a departure
but when is that moment?
can it be the top of the morning?
shall it be the mid of the day?
will it be lapped round
with a kaross of small hours?

I load my brain
with all manner of images
this quadrant and that

the whole sphere is spinning
this is sharper than science
input derives from a gut under tension
my bladder is full

brought up with fixed categories
I have fixated for years upon Europe
I am dancing now with Africa, place of my birth
who claimed me before I knew

is the place not opportune?
can the moment not be prescient?
'go go go' cries my mentor
'come come come' yell the folks

there is a twang of release
and ululation
can I put a girdle round the earth in search of my target?
shall I bring down my desired by noonday or by night?

GEOFFREY HARESNAPE

My Ma se Blues
(to Dyani, Mingus, and Miller)

First Voice:

Ma se favourite numbers were sharp sweet blue ones –

Second Voice:

Ninety-four   free each day lots and lots of
potable water for all that he loves
Two-thirteen   he lies for me on broken beer bottles
an' tries to squeeze out a drop of clean blood
Three-eleven   to hold together with pillars of bread
a collapsing heart, a dissolving brain –

First Voice:

Ja Allah… a lotta lotto tickets gotta save us today!

From depleted stars who blazed too far away, fierce
light   clear too bright drop on us
And so hate to brought it back   one night

Second Voice:

With heavily gyrating hips
Fate
Took my love's dream-filled head and
Crushed it between her legs

First Voice:

But here in the streets, where Hlumelo lies
Buried underneath tar – killed, reborn and
Killed again – each car roars off with my eyes

Second Voice:

Every truck grinds clean vision to dust to chuck
Across the sky the powdered jewel of my eye;
Each grain of memory grows to a burning pearl
Till the rattle of every speck that she now is
Quivers together the scrambled constellations
In a din conflagrates down on my head
And breaks open
Everything trapped inside of it

First Voice:

The N1 to Messina
Stole my only outjie away;
The N2 to Umtata
Took my bonny baby away;
Kom niewe-jaar, the South-easter
Blow them back to me again

Second Voice:

Twelve mouthfuls in heirdie box
Lasts een half-hour, cost thirteen bucks
And sometimes gets you fucked enough

Third Voice:

Even tho there's so much
My life must be used up in
I never regret
You one of the biggest.

So if tomorrow we dead
We'll have lived together
Lekker in our own harvest
And ate like pigs and drank

That water made us drunk
So much more than so much

All:

If you can't spare a one rand
Please give us a fifty cents –
If you won't give a one rand
Just throw us a fifty cents –
What, you think we never struggle
Just because we don't pay rent?

                    SIDDIQ KHAN

Song
(for Caragh)

The groan of the cars
The pulse of a flailing heart.
Wherever I go
The buzz of construction work.

I'm here but your tongue is still
In my mouth. Your teeth
That taste and feel as if
They were my own.

                     SIDDIQ KHAN

Prelude for Solo and Group Voices
(for Comrade Cronin and the residents of Soweto and Kaapstad)

He turned on the tap and sand coughed out it.
"We fought hard to drink water that wouldn't
poison us" *Out on the balcony, the mountain stared at him;
the air shook the world.* "To be honest doc,
I never felt anything but glad to be alive"
Two sentences, as if the First and Last:
"…when air channelled up the rock,
it cooled, condensed, and curdled into cloud –
thus the appearance of a white-grey tablecloth,
tumbling down the perpendicular slopes,
evaporating when it reached the floor…"
Struggle is not war.
"My lungs crumpled when our lives crashed
together,
but we are God when our clothes peel off"
Biting can be love.

"My suster was mos there at the confrins –
the big meeting between industry and govment;
she was one oda domestics that saw what happen'
when cleaning the pletnum toilettes det did hold the pee
oda Minsters and See-ee-ohs; she watched them choke
as one by one they ran to vomit
all the lekker dop, champ-pain and whatnot they suiped
turned to hot dry soil in their throats
an' made lumps of red clay with their spit."
He was not the only one; no, no, no – he was never alone.

SIDDIQ KHAN

Ubomi

Ubomu bunzima
Buzel'inkathazo
Bezel'inyembezi
Buphuphumal'izingqala nemimigqumo
Buzel'usizi
Olunzulu
Buzel'ubuhlungu
Obunganambaliso mntanasekhaya
Masomelele
Singalahl'ithemba
Mntakamama bubomi balonto
Bekezela

     NOSIPHO KOTA

Life

Life is hard
Full of troubles
Full tears
Burdened with overflowing sobs and roaring
Full of sorrow
The deep one
Full of pain
Too much of it my sibling
Let us be strong
And not lose hope
That is what life is about my sibling
Be strong

                          NOSIPHO KOTA
Translated by Zolani Prince Shapiro Tyalimpi

she imagines

his head would fit right into the bend of her elbow
where sticky skin is a creased page and his hair
a signature marked across that catches under her nails
she would look down at his head in a cradle to
see it thinned or grey and her own fingers soft with
washing liquid and years. at the

doorway she would still be with a slipper either
side of the glass had her forehead not witnessed each
   nights'
kiss above the steps with his back turned to the tea-lights
lighting the city to the indian ocean and the cargo ships
of women's limbs curling around a map he had
navigated a time before they met. but with

cool lips the forehead becomes irrational
a child too tired for bed but tired nonetheless
especially on saturday afternoons when poems don't
write themselves and visions of an extended arm with
two elbows at different angles and with two bodies
attached is easier to hope for. young too

with still so much to learn about what happens
behind the ribcage and to the spine when a finger becomes
tarnished by gold and how white really is not
at all but a dust sheet over water-stained furniture loved
by someone else who carved it faultless. in her

mind she takes a ferris wheel up to the tipping top
held back from falling by a rusted bar and
she waits to see each ride rode out by others played
in ones and twos some still with cowlicks and school-shoes
others with airport luggage. she sits

blue blanket hung to her knees with no pegs or hands to
keep it from slipping to her shins where a bruised picture
    of
silver high-heels with straps that snap and manicured
toenails pitches the scenery for an age she has tossed
    around
from the time she could first blow kisses.

LUISA LAGERWALL

the city

I

he took it out of his pocket.
unfolded it.
rested his mouth on the crease, but
for a moment too long.
then put it on the side table.

he stood at her window.
it's the city. he thought.
it's the dust. it's the cars at every stop street.

he moved his head down.
it moved too slow.
his eyes caught on the sheet with none of her.
sewn edge hemmed around.
tucked at the corners.

he sat on her bed.
it's the dent in her back. it's his fingers that don't fit.
it's the coat he bought, still unwrapped.
it's the city. he thought.

II

we'll be late,
he smiled. she took a photo.
and then another.
i have a gift for you.
but we'll be late.
he smiled. she went to answer the door.
his fingers tensed at his thighs.

and at the airport a plane was leaving.

III

are you sure?
it's the city, he said
i need to get out.

                        LUISA LAGERWALL

manning road

the white sun at 12 o'clock slows
their digging, sawing,
drilling. sirens of hadedas
behind the pawpaw tree suspend
in wonder the arms at work.

men in red overalls with rolled
sleeves up to the wrist, cup their hands
at the open tap all afternoon,
one after the other until the cement
is muddy and the day dug.

only knuckles of sweat drop
in the collapsing heat. brown fingers
over the grips of rusted wheelbarrows and
spades come back each morning
to wake the house.

LUISA LAGERWALL

The uncomfortable silence

The uncomfortable silence grows and grows like an over-
    eater in an easy chair   all oil-chinned and finger fat
    sick with tartrazine blue ankles and yellow-faced
the uncomfortable silence breeds like rats under the sofa
once started it cannot be stopped
it settles like dust that returns as soon as you sweep it
    away
it eats into faces and hearts   and it is always hungry

And the world waits for it to pass   the cars slow and the
    clocks stop
the waves still   and the winds die
stop   freeze   subside   and it is over

Bring the spinning saucers in   beam us up Scottie   and
    take us
away   deposit us elsewhere   in the large dark
    cavern of space

Make sure the Big Bang is still resounding   the waves
    still crashing the cars still driving   and the clocks still
    ticking
and we will be happy on our planet of sound

The uncomfortable silence of that blue speck once
    inhabited
will close in and swallow it   dry it out and crush it
    grind it down into dust   and scatter it to the dark

                                    JENNIFER LOVEMORE-REED

Ku Cindzuka ka Lwase

Rihlakahla i xihlungwani
Xo hlakahla naveto
Etimitswini ta mbilu;
Mbilu yi nga lwandle n'wamapfumala-ku-xurha.

Rihlakahla i lwase evuntshweni
Lebyi khameteke vampfompfomuri va ku:
Phyandlaphyandla a nala
*Tembenkulu a hundza!**
Va bvanyengetiwa hi min'wala ya tinsimbhi ta lwase
Ro valanga makhwati lama nuhaka rifu.

Lwase i khamera ya ntikelo, leyi kokaka no kurisa;
Ku rhurhumela ka swifuva swa xitshungu xa tintombi,
Ni ku kavanga no soholota ka vacini,
Swi yengetela ku ya phasiwa hi vurimba bya HIV/Aids.
Ohooo, hojomuu, egojini ro pfumala tshaku.

Lwase i ku dumela mihandzu leyi cindzukeke;
Mihandzu leyi nga phahliwangiki.
Lwase i ku khojometa nyama leyi byabyamaka;
Ivi n'wamakolo a ku: "Lexi nga nonisa nguluve a xi
    tiviwi!"
Kambe lexi xanisaka honci ha xi tiva;
I ku cindzuka ka lwasi evuntshweni.

*Lexi i xivuriso xa Varhonga loko va karhi va tluta va
    valanga hi swikwekwetsu swa nala.*

RISIMATI MATHONSI

The Ripening of Lust

Drooling is the climax
Of a crashing desire
In the heart's depths;
For the heart is but a voracious ocean
That never gets full.

Drooling is youth's lust
Which propelled the sailors to say:
Splash, splash!
Give way to Tembenkulu the pirate
The sailors are ambushed by lust's rough steel claws
Which roam in death-prone bushes.

Lust is a camera so potent –
With grand lens:
The bouncy bosoms of a bevy of girls,
And the fluttering and bendy dancers
Is greed's grim invitation to the HIV/Aids entrapment,
Oh, the fall into the deep bottomless pit.

Lust is but the rush to harvest green fruits,
Fruits not yet plucked off and tasted by the ancestors.
Lust is but the downing of blood-tender and bubbling meat,
And the lustful brags: 'What fattened a pig remains
    unknown!'
But that which troubles the boar is known –
It's the shameless consuming arrogance of the youthful.

RISIMATI MATHONSI
Translated by Vonani Bila

Ku Jayivha na N'wayingwani

Loko ti duma ti rara,
ti dikida pinyuluso ni nsoholoto wa swisuti
ni vacini va kwayito, mbaqanga ni phataphata,
va tiphata, va phahla hi ncino.
Va wachuta va hangalasa mavoko,
Va ndziwuluxa no swinya mahlo,
I xipinyapinya xa miehleketo ni naveto.
 Ndzi navela ku jayivha na N'wayingwani,
 Ndzi titlonya na ntsumi yanga,
Exifuveni xanga.

Ku mbvungunya ka jeze-xidzi,
Xirilo ni nkulungwani wa dzonga
swa Howling Wolf na Muddy Waters,
Ku vokotsa ka mhalamhala ya Miles Davis*
Ku qhavulela hi ku keta no konya
ka mpfurhetelo wa Jonas Gwangwa na Mackay Davashe
Aaah, ku pfilungana byongo ni naveto.
 Ndzi navela ku jayivha na N'wayingwani
 Ndzi titlonya na ntsumi yanga
Exifuveni xanga.

Yingisela vunanga
Bya ka mkhulu-wa-Ndongwe,
Ku tsemeka xinari xa Xinyori wa Mhlengwe wa xolwe ra katara,
Potoriyoo, potoriyoo, pototoo!
Ku sisimuka xihontlovila xa xidudla,
Xi haverile ku fana na Credo Muthwa
Xi nga nyimba ya ndhavuko werhu
I xandla famba, xandla vuya
Ndzi navela ku jayivha na N'wayingwani,
Ndzi titlonya na ntsumi yanga,
Exifuveni xanga.

Ndzi xicini, xigidavusiku ku kondza mahlambandlopfu a ku pfhaa!
Ndzi landze vahehemuki va kongome epuweni ra mali,
Endleleni ku fayeka mindzheko, xigugu na xigubu xa ndhavuko
Hikokwalaho ndzi ku ndzi tshikeni ndzi thlelela eka N'wayingwani,
Ndzi jayivha na ntsumi yanga,
Exifuveni xa xanga.

RISIMATI MATHONSI

Jive with N'wayingwani

When the music growls
And tickles the twisting waists
Even dancers of kwaito, mbaqanga and phataphata
Move poetically as they boogie
They twist and scatter hands
Eyes shut with glee
   I long to jive with N'wayingwani,
   Jive with my angel,
So tight in my bosom.

The soothing sounds of world jazz,
The sweeping blues and melodies of the South
Sounds of Howling Wolf and Muddy Waters,
The weeping of Miles Davis' trumpet,
The giggling, the clapping and growling
Of the bellowing melody of Jonas Gwangwa and Mackay
   Davashe…
   Aah, I long to jive with N'wayingwani,
   Jive with my angel,
So tight in my bosom.

Listen to the echoes from Mkhulu-wa-Ndongwe's sounds
The string of Xinyori the Hlengwe the guitar virtuoso
    cannot hold
Potoriyoo! Potoriyooo! Potoriyoo!
A stout man wakes from slumber,
Adorned like Credo Muthwa –
Bearer of our culture
And I say take it baby, give it to me!
    Aah, I long to jive with N'wayingwani
    Jive with my angel,
So tight in my bosom.

I'm the dancer –
I walk in the thickest night until the break of dawn,
I've traced the ways of exiles in the land of money
And on the way to freedom, they broke sacred calabashes
    and drums of tradition
    That's why I long to jive with N'wayingwani
    Jive with my angel,
So tightly in my bosom.

RISIMATI MATHONSI
Translated by Vonani Bila

Dithoto

Diphorogwana medingwana ya bontsi.
Malaola tsalano,
Matlhola kilano.
O thubile metse,
Kitlano e jelwe ke tlhwatlhwa.

Segwagwa se khumo–
Se a re goga-goga!
Kgobo-kgobo o re tagile
Re fetogile makgoba.
Re tsene dikgetsi tsa bangwe boteng,
Re ba laolela matshelo,
Re ba feketse,
Re ba wetse go khutlhe ka selelo.

Pelo e e tshwana ga ena manno,
Ka e tshela e kibitla.
Letseno le tsena letswa le tswapola letswalo,
Le tswatswailwa ke tuelo ya dithoto-malebatsa botho.

Dithoto ga o molato ka o supa katlego,
Mme go ba le bantsi o supa tshotlhego.
Kana go tlhoka dithoto go tlhola tlhobogo.
Seo ke bosilo ka lepotlapotla le jesa potsana.
Nako o mosenodi wa tshiamo–
Botshelo ke kago!

Bo Malema ba go epa khumo,
E ba bolaise ka makwalodikgang,
Go aname ditlhong,
Dikhumo tsa lepotlatlapotla di swabise.
Monna a tlaletlale teropo a itlhalosa.
Di mo kokonela dithoto tsa mekgwa ya mafifi.

Roma ga a agiwa ka letsatsi,
Boitshoko ga se boeleele,
Khumo ya lobelo e wetsa dingalo!

     KEA' MODIMOENG

Assets

Assets have become gods of many.
Ruining relationships,
Causing hatred.
Breaking families,
Unity has been bought by a penny.

Wealth and poverty –
Might be one tomorrow
We have become slaves of greed
We ruin people's lives
We cause them pain

Even our hearts have forgotten
Where to reside.
Our lives are valued in cash.
Assets have made us forget our humanity.

Assets show success,
Have done no wrong.
But too many are a show of lack,
For a lack of assets is a call to be forgotten.

The Malemas of this world dig for wealth,
And then adorn newspaper pages.
Causing shame across the land.
Instant wealth causes shame.
Causing men to explain themselves –
To tell what they did in the dark!

Rome was not built in a day,
Patience is no foolishness.
Instant wealth causes shame and pain!

>KEA' MODIMOENG
>*Translated by Sabata-mpho Mokae*

Ba lebetse batlhoki

Re ba sutela mebileng babusi ba tsela.
Ba ronoka ka mebala ya botala jwa loapi,
Bo tautona ka mabela.
Ga bana nako ba faraferwe ke mabaka,
Mabaka a a botlhokwa go feta batho.
Ba lebetse batlhoki.

Moranang re ba tlhopile go nna babusi,
Re ba neetse tlotla ya letshwao la tshepo.
Gompieno ke manong ba ja ka losika,
Ba gatela godimo, ke bo thutlwa.
Ba lebetse batlhoki.

Metseselegae e tlhanasela ka molelo,
Baagi ba fedile pelo go utlwala selelo.
Ba fisa gotlhe ba thuba tsotlhe.
Boitshoko bo kgadile,
Tlala e ba aparetse le mororo babusi bone;
Ba lebetse batlhoki.

Madi a tirelo sechaba a reka matlo-a-kgora,
Ga thumiwa mo ntsheng,
Go buiwa sekgowanyana.
Ba re ke bone fela ba lwela kgololesego.
Ba abelena ditiro ka botsala,
Ba lebetse batlhoki.

Bosenyi bo ile godimo,
Bodidi bo goroga ka mmetela.
Tokomane ya *Freedom Charter* e buisiwa ka matlhakore,
Fa o se wa "mokgatlho" o tla lala kwa ntle.
Dithuto tsa gago ga se sepe ntleng le "karata"
Ba lebetse batlhoki.

Ditsela di fetogile meepo,
Motlakase o rekwa ka kgomo.
Letseno le ngotlegile,
Lekgetho le oketsegile.
Ba ithobatsa kwa baipeing go ikutlwisa tlala
Morago ba tsamaele ruri,
Ba lebetse batlhoki.

Thekisho Plaatje robala boroko.
Ya lona tiro lo e dirile go sena di "thenda"
Lo kgaratlhile,
Lo agile!
Bangwe re tla gata metlhala ya lona,
Ere fa nako e tla re buse bagarona ka tolamo.
Ga jaana re tla lala ka ntho madi a tshologa,
Gonne:
Ba lebetse batlhoki, bo tau ba tletse dimpa!

KEA' MODIMOENG

They have forgotten the poor

We give them a right of way,
When they show off their blue lights,
The arrogant heads,
Who hardly have the time for us,
Having better things to do,
They have forgotten the poor.

In April we voted them to lead us
We gave them our mark of trust.
Today, they are vultures and only eat with their own.
Walking tall like giraffes,
They have forgotten the poor.

Townships are burning,
Tempers are flaring,
Residents burn and break everything,
Patience has run out,
Poverty has taken over, because the leaders
Have forgotten the poor.

The public purse is buying big houses,
They swim in liquor,
They speak in foreign tongues.
Because they are the liberation heroes,
They give each other positions,
They have forgotten the poor.

Crime has taken over,
Poverty is insulting our people,
Freedom Charter is read in bits and pieces,
Only members of the movement are in,
Papers are nothing without the card,
They have forgotten the poor.

Streets resemble mines,
Gas costs an arm and a leg,
Income has shrunk,
Tax has bloated,
They sleep a night at the squatter camps to taste hunger,
Then, they disappear forever.
They have forgotten the poor.

Rest in peace Thekisho Plaatje.
You did your work without "tenders".
You strove, you've built.
Some of us will step in your footsteps.
We shall govern our people with diligence when the time comes.
For now, we'll try to live with the pain,
Because
The lions' bellies are full.
They have forgotten the poor.

KEA' MODIMOENG
Translated by Sabata-mpho Mokae and Karabo Kgokong

Phamokate wa ratha wa fenetha
(Ho bao kaofela ba utlwileng bohloko ka baka la phamokate)

Lefu towe o mang o tswa kae.
Ebe mohlodi wa hao ke ofe ra tseba.
Hobane bo reyatseba ba o supa mona le mane.
Le ha ho ntse ho balwa balwa kokwana kgolo o fenetha
   ditjhaba.

Ma hemu hemu a re nneteng mohlodi wa hao ke bo mose
   ho mawatle.
Ha bo reyatseba bona ba re mohlodi ke tshwene tse tala tsa
   Aforika.
Nneteng mang ke mang eng ke eng.
Wena kokwana kgolo o tswetse pele o ya fenetha.

Jonna, kokwana kgolo wa tla wa ba sehloho.
O fenetha tjhaba tse nnyane le tse kgolo.
O fenetha bana le baholo.
O siya mahlomola le masisa pelo ho le ka kwano.

Phamokate wa tla wa ba kgopo ho ba kobo di kgutswhane.
Sheba kamoo o kakathang ditjhaba le batho ba
   futsanehileng.
Barui bona o phela nako e telle ho bona.
Empa ho bafutsana ka nakwana o ya fenetha hape o bolaye.

Aforika e ka tlase ho Sahara o e entse thakaneng ya hao ke
  moo o bapallang teng.
O e rathile ka selepe sa hao se sehloho empa ha o so tele.
O fithile bo Uganda o siile mahlomola.
Bana ba Aforika ba lla keledi tsa ba tsa omella marameng.

Lemong tsa ho feta o rathile Aforika ho tloha Bokone.
O theosa o ntse o ratha o repitla kokwana kgolo.
Kajeno o fihlile le Aforika e Borwa ka sebele.
Maafrika Borwa ha ba sa ho utlwa ka bare o fihlile wa
  repitla.

Jo, phamokate kannete ha o fihlile o sehloho ha o na
  ngwana e motle.
Bo reyatseba ba re tshwayetsano ya hao e feta ya lefatshe
  kaofela mona Aforika Borwa.
E be taba taba e be e leng Maaforika Borwa.
E be molato ke ho na ho hloka tsebo kapa ho sa mamele.

Re le setjhaba sa Aforika Borwa kannete le re tjhabetse.
Phamokate e re keneletse e ratha e moholo le e monyane.
Baheso re ya iponela phamkate ha e sa le tshomo e ya ratha.
F. fenetha tsatsi le hlahang le le dikelang.

Phamokate o sehloho kokwana kgolo.
Hobane o fenetha bo motswala ke ntse ke shebile.
O fenetha ba ahisane ke ntse ke shebile.
Kannete, wa tle wa fenetha setjhaba sa Aforika Borwa re
  ntse re shebile.

Re le setjhaba sa Aforika Borwa, ha re fetoleng boitshwaro
   ba rona ka thobalano.
Ha re hlokomeleng taba tsa marato le thobalano ya kae
   kapa kae.
Ha bao ba tshwanetseng ba hopole kgohlopo ha ba ya
   mapaeng.
Kannete, ha re sa fetole boitshwaro ba rona re le setjhaba,
   phamokate e tla re fenetha.

Hape phamokate o sehloho ebile o ntse o le moetsi wa
   matlotlo ho ba bang.
Ka ho le leng o siya ditjhaba di maketse di hlomohile.
Ka ho le leng ba bohlale ba iketsetsa matlotlo ka wena.
Kannete, phamokate wa kopakopanya jwale ka qalo ya
   mohlodi wa hao.

Phamokate nakong e kgolo le e nyane wa makatsa.
O bolaya bafutsana nakong e kgolo.
Empa barui bona ba ja ka wena.
"Sori", wa tle wa fetolwa bolo ya dipolotiki le kgwebo.

Phamokate wa tle wa o baka moferefere.
Hobane le bo tona kgolo ha ba tlameha ho botsa ka wena.
Ha ba batlisisa ba botsa ka wena e be ba se ba hatile noha
   mohatleng.
E be keng e na e kana e patwang ka wena phamokate
   kokwana kgolo?

                                    TSELA MOLOI

The rage of Aids
(To all who are affected by Aids)

Hey you cruel death.
Where do you come from?
Who gave birth to you?
When the seers are not even sure,
Even then you still destroy the nations.

Some say you come from over the seas.
Some blame the African baboon.
But who are you,
You who causes death and destruction?

Oh, how cruel can you be,
Killing small and big nations,
The young and the old,
Leaving heartache and pain.

Aids you are cruel to the poor.
See how you destroy the poverty-stricken.
Rich ones live longer,
But the poor ones you take away quickly.

Sub-Saharan Africa is your playground.
You have killed but you are still bloodthirsty.
You left them crying in Uganda.
Tears of Africa's children dry on their cheeks.

Years ago you killed Africa from up north.
You came down killing as you descend to the south.
Now you are rested in the south.
Even South Africans can feel your wrath.

Oh, Aids you are cruel indeed.
Some say that you kill more in South Africa than anywhere else.
South Africans what is the cause.
Is it because we don't listen.

The sun has gone down on us South Africans.
Aids is killing us across ages.
It is not a dream but a reality.
It kills day in and day out.

Aids you are cruel indeed.
You kill my cousin while I am watching.
You kill my neighbours in front of my eyes.
You kill South Africa while she is looking.

South Africans let us change our sexual ways.
Let us stop from sleeping around.
Let us remember condoms before we engage.
Otherwise Aids is going to finish us.

Aids you are cruel but you bring wealth to others.
Yet you leave nations in despair.
But wise ones make money out of you.
You leave me confused.

Time and time again you amaze me.
You kill the poor most of the time.
But the rich get richer through you.
"Sorry," became a political and commercial football.

Aids, you have caused us anguish.
For even the leaders must ask about you.
When they ask about you then all the hell break loose.
What is so big about you that must not be known?

TSELA MOLOI
Translated by Sabata-mpho Mokae

Thabure

Thabure pere tshweu pitsi ya Basotho.
E be sekoti sa hao ke se fe pitsi ya dithaba.
Hobane rona ba botjheng histori ya hao ha re e tsebe re ya
  e phopholetsa.
E be hantle ntle wena o mang pere tshweu.

Ha o thotse o itse tuu! hara mangau.
E be kemoo mangau a ileng a o qetella teng.
Hobaneng a ne a o qetella hodima thaba ya o na.
Moo e reng ha o le ka hodima yona e be o bona naha ka
  bophara.

Ba tsebang ba re o ne o rojwatswe ke kulo tsa maburu.
Le ha ba re kulo tseo tse o robaditseng di ile tsa fetoha
  metsi.
Kahoo ha wa robatswa ke dikulo o mpa o tshositswe ke
  magau.
O na a ileng a se ke a o thusa ha o ne o hlasetswe ke dira.

Pere tshweu wa robala bitleng la hao bohareng ba thaba ya
  mangau.
Wa shebahala o kgotsitse empa re tseba hantle hore ha wa
  robala ka kgotso.
Hobane naha eo o e shwetseng e sa le e ya le maburu.
Ke ka ho na o re tonetseng mahlo re le ditloholo tsa hao.

Mayibuye ha le kgutle lefatshe pitsi ya naha.
Hobane ha wa roballa lefela la mafela thabeng ya mangau.
Kannete, o e lwanne Thabure ha re nkeng moo o siileng ha le kgutle lefatshe.
Robala ka kgotso pitsi ya bahlabane, mme re tla sala re e lwana ho ya ho ile!

                                          TSELA MOLOI

Thabure

Thabure the white horse of the Basotho.
Tells us which hole is yours.
We the younger ones do not know your story.
Tell us who you are

Why are you so quiet among the cheetahs?
Is that how the cheetahs have eaten you.
Why haven't they finished you up on that mountain?
So that you can see who lands from above

Those who know say the bullet from a Boer rifle ended
    your life.
Even though they say the bullet turned to water,
You were not put to sleep by the bullet but the cheetahs,
Which did not help you when enemies came for you.

White horse take your rest in that grave.
In the middle of the cheetahs' mountain
You look so peaceful.
But we know that your rest is not peaceful.
For the land you died for is still theirs.
That is why we are looking at you.

Mayibuye
Let your land come back to you wild horse
For you did not die in vain on that mountain of the
    cheetahs.
Yes you have fought, Thabure.
We will carry the baton.
Rest in peace warrior horse,
We will carry the baton!

TSELA MOLOI
Translated by Sabata-mpho Mokae

For Your Drinking Pleasure

Our special limited edition Pinotage
With a deep vibrant ruby hue
It's acidic?
My apologies kind Sir, I'll get another bottle
Perhaps the woman who picked the grapes was sick that day

A vintage bottle aged in oak
With a sweet taste of juicy layered ripe fruit on the palate
Sour?
I am so sorry; let me get you another one
Maybe she was sad that day because she gave birth in the vineyard

A rare and mature variety
With a blend of aromatic silky tannins
Oh no, bitter you said?
Please pardon me I'm sure the next one will be better
It could be her husband had been mistaken for a baboon and killed

A full-bodied unique wine
With a spicy essence on the nose
It stinks, really? Ruined your day?
I beg your forgiveness, honourable gentleman
You see her life was ruined when she was evicted and made homeless

JACKIE MONDI

List of Sound Effects

I.

Bare feet
across his heart when he stood still to listen.

II.

The moon
emptying a bowl of ashes into the back garden.

III.

A broom
sweeping up the pieces of a calamity from the kitchen
    floor.

IV.

The spring
protesting all winter on the old caliper of his shoe.

V.

Yellow pages
flapping from a broken dream about the wind.

VI.

The sun
sliding behind the line of plane trees all along his
   childhood.

VII.

A small
animal running on a wheel in the dead of night when all
   else is still as a grave.

VIII.

The grave
of his father slowly growing over with long grass and
   weeds

in the Mountain Rise Cemetery.

KOBUS MOOLMAN

Eight Critical Questions

Ask her.

Ask her   if the smoke stings /

Ask her   if the flames change colour as they burn through the six layers of her skin /

Ask her   if she knows when the smell starts /

Ask her   at what point burned skin stops feeling anything /

Ask her   if she knows the price of any of the following:
- half a litre of petrol
- a box of Lion matches
- an old car tyre
- several fist-sized stones for throwing /

Ask her   if she knows how they turn bone into powder in an incinerator /

Ask her   how long it takes teeth to break down /

Ask her   if heads can grow back, like a lizard's tail /

Ask her.

Ask her if she saw anyone else that day.

KOBUS MOOLMAN

His Explanation
in which the stones of the earth fail to make a sound.

She wants to go to the cemetery again
to visit his grave. And I (who have a car) will take her.

We won't spend long
because it isn't safe in the cemetery anymore.

She'll carry water in a plastic milk bottle
and a packet with kitchen scissors and a bunch of white
    carnations.

We won't spend long
because what else is there to do

after she's changed the flowers and
cleared the white stones of weeds and encroaching grass?

She'll stand a moment
bent over in silence holding on to the headstone.

And, of course, she'll weep.
But that's all.

And then we'll go,
keeping the doors locked and looking around us all the
    time.

There really isn't much to it.
I don't know why the others aren't prepared to help.

                              KOBUS MOOLMAN

Runaway

Beneath the freeway underpass
running to Isipingo Beach
three young boys balance
on the edge of the N2
in thin t-shirts their fathers
once bought them.
Two holding backpacks,
one swinging a Checkers packet.

At night they walk along
the old railway tracks,
listening to the wind
carry cars home.

They pass the canal
lit by steel factories' silent smoke.
In Prospecton they hustle maache
running from security guards.

At Rivermouth they flake off
ashy meat at the brick-braais,
pick up empty beer bottles
and head into the mangroves.

Beneath the freeway underpass
running to Isipingo Rail
three young boys sleep
at the edge of the N2.
Two holding backpacks,
one kicking in his sleep.

DASHEN NAICKER

O a ipona

O a ipona ebile ga a bone gore o ya kae yo motho,
Ga a bolele segagabo o re o ja sekgowa o re ke tsela,
Ke lekgowa le leswana ke kgoa o ganana le botho,
Motho ke yena batho ga se bona yena o a sela.

O se kwetenketša a šinyaletše a tsopola bangwadi,
A se phethola a se phaphatha ka leleme ba tshetshetha,
A se famoletše dinko a se thuntšha pele ga batswadi,
O a se opediša, o a se bolediša, o a se retha.

Ke monyatši o na le lenyatšo o nyatša tšohle le bohle,
O nyatša balemi le bahlagodi o re ga ba šome ke dikwefa,
Ke molebadi o lebala ge a nameletše ka bona,
O lebala gore ke poo a ka patišwa ka lefagolo a golola ka
   kefa.

Šo lehono ga se mo enywetše dienywa sekgowa,
Ba mo lobile ka malwa a lebala a phirimelwa.

PULENG NKOMO

He is full of himself

He is full of himself he doesn't see where he is going,
He is not speaking his language and only uses English and
    says it is *the* way,
He is a black white man he is a bully he hates humanity,
He is *the* man; others are nothing, he is fending for
    himself.

He is fluent, pulling faces and quoting the writers,
He capsizes it, pats it with the tongue while they trot,
Nostrils wide open, shooting it in front of his parents,
He is conducting it, making it audible, racing it,
    brandishing it.

He is disrespectful he undermines everyone and
    everything,
He undermines farmers and weed removers and says they
    are prisoners,
He forgets that he is who he is because of them,
He forgets that he can be attacked and cry to them for
    help.

Here he is today; his English is not bearing him any fruits,
They lost him to alcohol and he forgot to go home.

                                           PULENG NKOMO
                                    Translated by Mpho Molapo

Ga gešo mekgotheng

Tago la ka ke tla le botša mang,
Ge phelo bja ka bo fetogile leswiswi?
Ke mang a ka khorišang pelo ya ka,
A khoriša pelo ya ka ka lerato le borutho?

Ke tsoga phoka di sa wele ke nyaka difihlolo,
Mosegareng wa sekgalela ke hlehla le mekgotha,
Ke tseba mo go jago bahumi le ba go jela go khora,
Mašadiša le mare a bona ke boipshino bja ka.

Ke beilwe ka tlase ga kgatelelo ke mabaka,
Ga se nna mohlami wa koša ya bophelo,
Eupša ke moopedi wa yona; ke opela ka megokgo,
Ka nako ntšu la ka le ganelela magalagapeng.

Ke mpša ke se mpša ke fetošitšwe go ba bjalo,
Ke gopola ka sehlogo sa bophelo e se ka boomo,
Eupša e le ka baka la boima bjo ke lebanego nabjo,
Tšatši ka tšatši, bošego ka bošego ke lwa ntwakgolo.

Ke rakedišwa ke tsogo la molao ge ke leka maano,
Ga go yo a mphago sebaka sa go hlaloša phelo bja ka,
Ke fošwa ka melamo le maswika bjalo ka lehodu,
Godimo ga hlogo ya ka go lla molongwanamoswana.

Ke tšwele mekhino ke sa le ngwana ke sa senya selo,
Mmele wa ka ka moka ke magotšane boka gopane,
Pula tša dikgadima le dikapoko di ipshinne ka nna,
Marega ke welwa ke phefo tša mehuta di ntsena marapong.

Ke mang a ntirilego gore ke be moagi wa mokgotheng?
A hleng dikubu le dikwena di tseba madiba a tšona?
A hleng dinonyana tša lefaufau di tseba dihlaga tša tšona?
Ke reng ke bakišana madulo le diphepheng le dinoga?

Ge ke bona bana ba bangwe ba sepela le batswadi ba bona
Nna pelo ya ka e rothotha ka boima e rotha madi a dihlabi,
Ke dihlabi tše ntlhabago moya le maikutlo di nkuka di nkhudua,
Di nkgopotša lerato ke le hlokilego phelong bja ka bja dillo.

Ee, le ge go le bjalo ke tla ema ka ikemiša le nna – a e ka se be mafelelo,
E ka se be mafelelo a ka, ke tla ema ka namelela, ka namelela marung,
Ke tla ema ka obelela le nna; ke tla swara naledi ka diatla ka e bea hlogong,
Tago la ka e ka se hlwe e e ba la sephiri le bogoboga gape le dihlong.

Le nna ke tla phadima ka phadimela tšhaba sešo le bešo,
Mekgotha ke tla e fetoša dikgoro le mafapa a tirelo le thuto,
Mekgotha ke tla e fetoša manamelelo a ba hlokišitšwego sebaka,
Ke tla e fetoša diipone tša boitshenko tša setšhaba sa molalatladi.

PULENG NKOMO

In my neighbourhood

Who will I shed my light to,
When my life has formed into darkness?
Who will fill my heart,
And fill it with love and warmth?

I wake up at dawn, and scrounge for food,
During the day I wander in the neighbourhood,
I know where the rich, fat-bellied ones eat,
Their left-overs and saliva are my delight.

I've been pressurised by situations,
I'm not the composer of the song of life,
I am but its singer; I sing it with tears,
Oft-times my voice refuses to come out of my throat.

I am a dog while I am not a dog, I have been made to be so,
I think of the cruelty of life not by intention,
But because of the heavy burden I am carrying,
Day and night I'm fighting a huge battle.

I'm being chased by laws when I try my tricks,
No one gives me a chance to explain my life situation,
I'm being thrown at with knobkerries and stones like a thief,
On my head there are gunshot sounds.

I'm gap-toothed though still young but I haven't done
    anything wrong,
My body is full of cracks like a skunk,
Thunderstorms and fogs have turned me into their toy
In winter, different winds befall me and pierce my bones.

Who made me a neighbourhood wanderer?
Hippos and crocodiles know their home,
Birds flying high in the sky return to their nests,
Why do I have to fight for shelter with scorpions and snakes?

When I see other children with their parents,
My heart beats heavily with pains,
Pains which stab my soul and feelings shake me,
Reminding me of the love I never received in my sorrowful life.

Yes! I will stand on my two feet – this will not be the end,
It will not be the end of me; I will stand up and rise, rise above the sky.
I will rise and incline towards; I will take the star with my bare hands and put it on my head.
My light will no longer be of secrecy, disgrace and shame.

I will shine and shine for my nation and family,
I will change the neighbourhood into service and education sectors,
I will change the neighbourhood into a stepping stone of those who were denied opportunities,
I will change it into mirrors of introspection for the rainbow nation.

PULENG NKOMO
Translated by Mpho Molapo

Natla tša ntwa ya tokologo

Oliver Tambo…

Bagale le bagaleadi ba tšhaba sešo,
Re ka lebala bjang bogale le bonatla bja lena,
Lena mailagofenywa malwelatoka le tokologo?
Re ka lebala bjang madi le kudumela tša lena,
Lena mailagoinama la gana se le tshela sa ditshehla?

Lilian Ngoyi…

Bagale le bagaleadi ba tšhaba sešo,
Re ka lebala bjang mahloko le megokgo
Malapeng a lena ge le be le tšwele ka difata?
Ba robilwego maatla ba dutše hlakahlakamatete.
Re ka lebala bjang tsepu tša lena bagale le bagaleadi?

Nelson Mandela…

Bagale le bagaleadi ba tšhaba sešo,
Re ka go lebala bjang wena Madiba, nywaga ya phelo bja
   gago,
Nywaga ye e tletšego lehutšo la tokologo ya bana ba batho?
Ga sa ka wa kgetha mmala, o hlaotše kgethologanyo,
Wa e šupa bjalo ka lepheko, wa gana kgatelelo ya botho le
   setho.

Dijamollo…

Bagale le bagaleadi ba tšhaba sešo,
Re ka lebala bjang boikgafo bja lena?
Lena le emego setia la gafa phelo bja lena,
Re ka lebala bjang madi a tšhologilego ka 1976?
A tšhologilego pele ga molomo wa sethunya.

Madira a rumo la setšhaba…

Diaduma tša legodimo di ka kgakgana ratadimeng,
Sasedi le tšokotšane tša bophelo di ka rutla ka bogale,
Noka di ka ela tša gopa, mawatle a kgelempua ka maphoto,
Pula tša medupi le matlakadibe tša na wa kaparelanaga,
Ee, re tla le gopola ka nagakgomo ye le e lwetšego.

Putswa tša banna le basadi…

Le tšwa kgole thipa di sa ja bagale ka bogale swiswing,
La swara mollo ka diatla, godimo ga meetse la o gotša,
La lwa ka dikonaona, la lwa ka marumo, la lwa ka tšohle,
La gana go lalwa ke kgang sera se le hlomere la se hlohlora,
La hlomola naga mootlwa mahube gwa khukhuša a
    tokologo.

Bo sele bo hlahlametše…

Šemo lehono re setšhaba se tee sa malementši,
Re a bolela, re a *bua*, re a *bolabola*, re a *thetha*, re a *khuluma*,
Ga re hlaole *ons praat* ebile *we talk* re sa metše le mare,
Tswetla gaRamapulana ge re fihla re a *amba* ra amogelwa sešate,
Re setšhaba se tee sa ditšontši re bopetšwe go jelana tšelane gotee!

Setšhaba gare ga ditšhaba…

Re setšhaba sa mohlolo, setšhaba sa mohlala wa go hlalala,
Mmala ga e sa le lepheko ga e sa le swao la karoganyo,
Kgethologanyo re e kgabeletše ka sa magagane sa therišano,
Ya bana ba thari mešomo ga e sa le go goga le go kgorometša,
Ga e sa le go kuka le go rwala, šuposegolo ke tirišano le kabelano.

Le e lwele…

Le e lwele le hlabane tlhabano mehlala ya lena še pele ga rena,
A go rene šebešebe, khutšo le lekepekepe di ikepele go rena,
Tlhako ya morago a e gate mo ya pele e gatilego ka seriti,
Go fele pako ya maemo le megabaru, bohle re ngwathišaneng.
Ka tumelo tša rena tša maphaaphaa a re rapeleng thapelo e tee ya khutšo!

PULENG NKOMO

Heroes of war of freedom

Oliver Tambo…

Heroes and heroines of our nation,
How can we forget your braveness and heroism?
You who refuse defeat; the fairness and freedom fighters,
How can we forget your blood and sweat?
You who refuse to be defeated by the pale one's system.

Lilian Ngoyi…

Heroes and heroines of our nation,
How can we forget the grief and tears at your homes when you were away?
Others were powerless, living in the island of wonders,
How can we forget the foundation you made, you heroes and heroines?

Nelson Mandela…

Heroes and heroines of our nation,
How can we forget you, Madiba, the years of your life?
The years full of hope for freedom of sons and daughters of man,
You never discriminated against colour, you separated racism,
And pointed it as an obstacle, and refused the oppression of humanity.

Fire eaters…

Heroes and heroines of our nation,
How can we forget your devotion?
You who stood your ground and sacrificed your lives,
How can we forget the blood shed in 1976?
Shed before the pipe of the gun.

Warriors of the spear of the nation…

The heavenly storms are in conflict in the sky,
Whirlwinds and life shakers can raze with power,
Rivers can flow and erode; seas overflowing with waves,
Gentle rains and thunderstorms can cover the land,
Yes! We will remember you on the mighty country that
    you have fought for.

PULENG NKOMO
Translated by Mpho Molapho

Soekers

Soek en jy sal vind
net God se liefde is blind.

Heer, ek het gesoek na U
in die eens vredige vars oggendlug,
Ek het gesoek na U stem
in die sedelose stiltes
wat voor die soekers vlug

maar Heer,
U is nie meer daar
nie in die oggendlug vol rook,
nie in die rustelose geraas
van soekers wat in hul haas
vergeet van U my Heer.

Heer, ek soek nog dag-na-dag.

Ek soek na U grootsheid
in die stukkie hemel
deur my venster,
hier in my hok vannag
waar die lig van slapende sterre
my nie kan bereik,
waar drome van dit wat was
nie meer wil wyk.

Heer, ek het gesoek
en ek het gevind,
ons soekers bly steeds blind

MARTHA PRETOORS

Seekers

Seek and you will find
only God's love is blind.

Lord, I sought You once
in the peace of fresh morning air.
I sought Your voice
in the lawless silence
before the seekers flight

but Lord,
You're no longer there,
not in the smoky morning light,
not in the restless noise
of seekers in their haste
who've forgotten You, my Lord.

Lord, still day-by-day I seek.

I seek your grandeur
in the piece of heaven
coming through my window,
here in my nightly cage
where the light of sleeping stars
doesn't reach,
where dreams of what was
refuse to leave.

Lord, I looked
and yet I find
that seekers remain blind.

MARTHA PRETOORS
Translated by Liesl Jobson

Verlore beeltenis

Al wat ek oorhet
is 'n ou vergete foto van jou.

Ek betas nog elke dag
die sagte lyne
van jou sielvolle oë,
die weerloosheid
van jou sagte mond.

Elke oomblik
bekyk ek jou perfekte beeltenis –

Tot dit vir my verlewendig,
tot die warm lig
van jou oë
wakker word
en tot dit voel
asof jou glimlag
... net vir my bestaan.

        MARTHA PRETOORS

Lost Picture

All that's left
is an old, forgotten photo of you.

Daily still I recall
the gentle lines
of your soulful eyes,
the defencelessness
of your soft mouth.

Every moment
I stare at your perfect image –

until I am enlivened
and the warm light
of your eyes
comes alive
and it feels
as if your smile
exists for me alone.

> MARTHA PRETOORS
> *Translated by Liesl Jobson*

After Battiss

My father was a waterfall, my mother a butterfly. – Walter
 Battiss

My father was an ocean
   in thrall to the moon
My mother was a crab
   earthbound carapace

My sisters are swimming waves
   rolling up to break
My brother is wide sand
   sharpened underfoot

My friends are my friends
   penguins closely packed
   clumsy in crowds, perhaps,
   but sleek when they swim

And small girl is beached snail
   digs in while the tide goes out

        GILLIAN RENNIE

I Remember Bethesda

I remember dubbeltjies, donkeys that let themselves into
   the garden at night, and the sudden breeze death
   carries in its careful arms;
I remember how bruised the skin of the sky gets before a
   storm breaks away from it.

I remember the punch of winter frost, and the tickle of
   stars on black velvet just before;
I remember the plovers, banging their busy tools around
   Elise's dam; and hoopoes facing the ground, fussy old
   women in feathers;
and I remember how the river could roar like the sea.

I remember Rolene, checking on the church; and Stirling,
   walking to the two-kilometre mark.
I remember fairy cloths, laid on the grass early on April
   mornings; and Daisy when she was fleet.
I remember 1066 and 1948, and the barn that everyone
   wants to buy,
and I remember sweet shade under heavy trees.

I remember cats sleeping on the job in the trading store,
   and Alta's birds lecturing the deaf afternoon;
I remember the smell of garlic being sorted; and the
   heaviness of rotting pears on the air.
I remember tourist season, when visiting dreams flowered;
and I remember how local threshers reaped the coins from
   every crop;

I remember cycling with Debbie, swimming in the bend
   of the river, and seeing a tortoise.
I remember cycling past snakes, and feeling the silence of
   a heart in space.
I remember watching the poplars turn, the clouds move,
   and the cottage under Rendo's trees dissolve.

I remember moth wings in the morning.

I remember pure air, and the way it could whip your
   cheek.

And I remember that, some days, all this could hurt.

GILLIAN RENNIE

Your Heart was a Squatter-Camp

Your heart was a squatter-camp:
shebeen-happy; collage-torn
a sullen mash in winter
criminally torpid in summer.

With enough wood and sticks
and cardboard
anyone could set up home there:
the post-office clerk
the accountant in Claremont
the woman who sold the Big Issue at
the Newlands traffic lights.

Up one day, down the next.
We your children
lived in constant fear of eviction.
We feigned indifference, swishing past
like BMWs on the N1
or the airbusses taking off overhead
that grazed
– in passing –
the thin air your heart kept gobbling up
and pushing out again.

                    BEVERLY RYCROFT

Has your Dad got a bird yet?

Unlike these scabbed city hoboes
my father's pigeons were of royal blood:
purple
broad-throated
burbling
they were the aristocrats the
eugenic athletes bred to
find their way back from anywhere.

Saturday afternoons
the phone would herald their approach
from lookouts in
Middledrift
Grahamstown
Queenstown and
Hotazel

"Has your Dad got a bird yet?"

And it would be get the washing
off the line get off the bladdy phone
can't you see I'm waiting for a bird
you idiot stop waving that stick around
the back yard
bugger off
get inside
the lot of you.

Alone in the back yard
Dad's narrowed eyes would counter
blue with blue
aiming like ack-ack guns until
he located
long before the rest of us
(bunched at the kitchen window),
the suspended mark
the small, obscure punctuation
the blue void would eventually
cough up for him

and dangle
between teasing fingertips.

a bird

swivelling and soaring coolly
once
twice
in casual victory laps around the loft.

And Dad outside the loft rattling
a feed tin and
whistling feverishly to bring it in
and Mom inside the house snorting:
nobody can whistle and swear
at the same time
Can they?

That was thirty years ago but I still
keep going
back and back to the places of home

and even my dreams
are Olympian, shimmering-throated birds
that fly in from foreign cities
to peck at the windows
of empty houses and search
in the feeders
of abandoned lofts.

                              BEVERLY RYCROFT

The wind at Uilenskraalmond

If the wind wears me down, peels me skin and pith
If the wind pops my fingers and knee caps
If it papers past membrane and wipes fluid
If the wind tears my hair and scatters it northsouth
If the wind pulls my nails and bends my neck
If it dries my eyes nose mouth
If the wind shakes heart liver
If it rattles skull
If it blows and cures
If it shears
If it scours me need-clean
If it sings my bones
If the wind wastes nothing wants nothing waits for nothing
If the wind browses the museum of my body
If it is the wind
It is this wind.

KARIN SCHIMKE

Robben Island: Museum in the Making

Everything here is reminiscent of the dead.
White cross near the shore,
Whale bone propped grotesque against the moon,
An ostrich, hollow-eyed, flesh still stubborn on the bone.
Sky blue empty mussels pattern
Shells of spiky brown, white and pink,
Glint of silver, gleam of pearl.
A penguin stark in black and white
Died intertwined in shining weeds.

Rocks like gravestones dot the shore
Marking debris from ship and city life
Which scream their rottening presence:
Plastic bottles, left-footed Chinese sandal,
Rope and plank, blue hair slide,
Crayfish skulls, all whitening in the sun
While the segregated graveyards

For maddened lunatics, 'leper' patients and
The poorest of the poor,
All swallowed up in bush.
Those for Commissioner Thompson
And the lighthouse-keeper's wife,
Who died at thirty-eight,
Are cordoned off in stone
And churchyard children's graves
Speak sadly of their tender age.

Army building T225
Dank, dark, stinking.
Rusted doors, tight against the eye.
A broken window offers
coffin structures built rigid in cement
and an orange picture in the gloom.
Perhaps the picture of a man
Pointing straight his gun.
A lone grey pigeon guards a sill.

The mountain merely watches
As she always has.
Convicts and slaves,
Her own free men of men,
Wardens, prisoners, commissioners, visitors,
All those who passed along
This dusty road to stare
And dream at her
She offers comfort.

Roads of empty wardens' houses
Devoid of smiles or laughter
Cupboard doors agape
Artificial red carnation
Pinned against a wall.
No sign of any pictures
One left over poster

About two dogs sleeping in your mouth
And a blanket left behind.
Shell encrusted gardens
Proud strelitzia trapped inside
A tiny concrete pot
Its bird-shaped flowers
Stifled at the root.

The clubhouse has a dungeon,
A Visitors' Book with curses
And dreary tales of drunken decadence.
The Mess is dark and heavy
Closed tight against the sea,
And in the pub, the bar
Obscures the open sky.

Inland, a hibiscus tree
Festooned with blazing blossoms,
Lives off some dripping water.
A lone tomato plant twists upward
In constructed beds of gravel.
And parsley, fresh and green,
Still growing near a broken door.

And yet

Two tortoises round and mottled
That reach up almost to my knees
Are imprisoned in a tiny yard
They have eaten all the grass
Excreted coagulated bowling balls
Of straw that dry dark brown in the sun.
They park against the wire fence
Reptile necks protruding, black eyes questioning
Sniffing free air through the mesh.

Barbed wire prison walls
Where dripping sand
in a prisoner's hand
Was hopeful
Where learning came from cement bag books
And where the human spirit
Thrived.

And so
I drink a daily dose of Table Bay
Savour the stillness of the air
Hold on to the image of a tomato plant
Still growing
There are gardens waiting to be planted
A whole island waiting for new growth.

MAVIS SMALLBERG

Remembering prisons and prisoners

I. Robben Island

For decades you were a distant, quiet mound
resting in the icy Atlantic like a dormant whale.
Often I glanced at you from the corner of my eye,
winding down *De Waal* to the heart of the city.

History books and oppressors defined you –
prison of terrorists, Mandela and Sobukwe.
I learnt that Tuan Guru & other meddling princes
from the Tidorean archipelago, submitted there too.

Today, I stand in the dreaded quarry
where defiance broke rocks, building bastions
for the *broederbond*. It's hard to conceive
captive comrades countering such brutality.

Your rugged beauty celebrates resistance.
Surreal seagulls sweep across your chaste lines,
soar through flung spray, scattering glistening
beads between me and an azure sky.

I finally witness the reclining lion, majestic, powerful.
Hollow prisons which isolated resilient souls,
the indomitable cruelty of oppression enrages.
Anguish is still tactile in the interrogating rooms.

Outside, on the lawn, a blonde photographer
eagerly coaxes a black sculptor and his artifact
to attain symmetry for her contrived composition.
Feigned postures border on the sacrilegious.

I observe recorder & subject negotiating,
neither settling the score of this delicate dance.
Yet this simple usurpation of your hallowed ground
made me wonder about your future:

Now that we can saunter on your sacred sands
what intricate games of power will we witness?
Who will interpret your past? Through whose lens
will your pilgrims view you in the new democracy.

II. Remembering

Remembering Chicago & the budding season,
when we spoke of impending winter
here, in the aftermath of dry spells
in the divided country.

In the twilight of the fecund era
down at The Cape of Storms
hungry black men deliberate,
stare at crumbs, frugal menus of cunning bosses –
bald, desperate demagogues
snatching burning legacies.
They lick their scalded fingers crying:
We didn't know. We're sorry.

The bones immortalise another story:
Goniwe, Calata, Sparrow.

All this happened somewhere before –
was it in sunny California?

Remembering an old white social worker in Illinois
watching a film about Japanese prisoners
in the brutal Belsens of America –
I heard those words again:
I'm sorry. I was there, but I didn't know.

Remembering this morning, the television screaming
a prelude to a sinister soapie:
Don't buy Honda, Toyota or Mazda.
Try American, Buy American
And may the best car win!

Should we remember, turn the other cheek,
forgive and forget old, foolish men?

III. Prisoner

he waited –
on the steps, above the crowd
solemn, contemplative
Jumu'ah had ended.

he spoke –
miss prison
don't think you need a house
& everything else that goes with it

he clarified –
don't want to return to jail
but yearn for the solitude
freedom to talk to the Almighty

he urged –
come and visit soon
I
shall give you
Allah's protection.

      ABU BAKR SOLOMONS

Lovuka lelosiko

Kobe kusempondo zankomo
zethu thina banumzane ngokunumuza,
Ilanga lobe selikhotha
Izintaba empumalanga,
Kuqala nobuhle bosuku olusha,
lwaphakade naphakade.

Sovuka konke sekushintshile,
Yeb impumalanga nentshonalanga,
kobe kusenjengoba,
Ubuthina bethu bodwa,
obuyobe sebushintshile,
Bavuka bama ngazozimbili.

Sobe sonke sesiphendukile,
Sazi khumbul'ubuthina bethu,
Izinkolo zethu namasiko,
Sekubuye ngezinkani,
Nathi sesizazi ukuthi,
Singobani bakaBani.

Sokhomba enonile,
esibayenikazi esinyinyitheka
ezimpemvu,indl'ivaliwe namalanda,
Sihlabe simemeze 'idubukele'
Kubuye uwonkewonke kufinywe ngendololwane.

Yek' amabheshu nezinjobo ukuyikazela,
Yek' amayikayika izidwaba,
Yek' abafana ukuzibuyis' inhlazane,
Yek' ukukleza kwegwansile,
Yek' izaqheqhe ukuqhilika emaguleni,
Sekuphelile ukusenga ezimithiyo ngobuthina.

Izinxuluma zovuka,
Vumbu njengamakhowa,
Imithombo iyogobhoza,
Imifula nayo ihaze uhazane,
Kube mtoti kudele kwelikaphunga.

Konke kobe sekushintshile,
Inkungu seyisukile,
Namehlo esevulekile,
Silungise imuva lethu
esalilahla kudalo,
Sicabele ikusasa indlela,
Eya phambili kwaNompumelelo,
Sivuse naleli siko.

Yeka lezozicoco ukuthungwa,
Nazicholo ukukhehlwa,
Izintombi ukushingila,
Nazinsizwa ukuyokhuzela,
lena ezansi emithonjeni.

Bakhapheyana beyokleza,
Mantombazanyana ayotheza,
emahlanzeni ayob'eseyiwo
phansi kuChozomane neGodlwayo
izintaba zangakithi.

Sobophela uhide lwezinkabi,
Siyoklama izindimakazi
zakwethu le phansi kwaSivukuvuku.
Inqeke yeka
Amabhece wona we!
Umbila namaswela ke
Wo he! lobe selibuyile lelosiko
lethu esalilahla kudalo.

Ke sithole nethuba
lokubhula amahawu,
asalala izintuli kudalo,
Sishwilinganise izikhwili,
Sidavuze ngelikhulu iwala,
Siqonde ngqo koNozibanibani
Ingani zobe zenda ,zemula,
kunomsindo,kusindwe ngobethole,
Wo! yeka ubuthina bethu ukuvuka madoda
namasiko ethu ukuma mpo.

                    BHEKANI THABEDE

Tradition Awakens Again

At the break of dawn,
The sun will rise up in
the eastern mountains,
A new day will dawn,
Forever.

As we awaken, all will have changed,
Yes, East and West will remain the same,
But our origins will rise again.

All will change and remember
our values and roots,
We shall know who we are,
Where we come from and most of all,
Where we are going.

We shall rejoice in a feast,
As everyone will come and feast with us.

Yes our cowhide attire,
Yes our headgear,
Yes the cream from the milk in the calabash,
Will reveal the truth about who we are,
Our origins.

The mountains will rise again,
The wells will overflow again,
The rivers will surge again,
Yes the beauty of our land
will once again be known.

All will change,
Dawn will break,
Our eyes open again,
We will be fixing our past,
Which we forsook long ago,
We will carve a new way forward,
To the road of success,
Awakening our traditions in the process.

Headgear fit for king will be sewn again,
The maidens will parade,
The young men will dance,
Down by the riverside.

The maidens will gather wood,
Up in the mountains of Cholomane,
And Godlwayo,
Our heritage mountains.

Our livestock will surround our,
Territory in KwaSivukuvuku,
The mealies, pumpkins and melons,
Will be in abundance,
Yes our culture will be reclaimed,
Which we forsook long ago.

Opportunity to our sticks and shields,
Which had gathered dust will again be upon us.
We shall wave them in song as we march forward,
To Noziboniboni,
In great anticipation,
Weddings, coming of age ceremonies,
Will be galore as we gather to
Feast and celebrate who we are,
And our legacy shall stand erect
Once again.

BHEKANI THABEDE
Translated by Nomphumelelo Sibongile Sithole

Trampled

Winter confronts the Cape
of Good Hope
with a snarl, barking
her dog breath
over the peninsula.

At Fish Hoek
a canvas recliner waves
its red stripes – warning
the spring tide
as it laps up yesterday's
footprints from the sand.

Next to the hole
where your floral umbrella
pierced the skin of the beach,
a single print – the heel cut deep,
question marks empty space
where our towels lay
side-by-side.

A charred cloud,
etched into grey, growls
while biting into remnants
of sun, and spitting
I unroll my raincoat
while your bulldog
still begs for a bone

        CHRIS VAN DER WALT

For Maria Pilar

It's enough…
I watch you as we navigate,
there are no stars,
a groundswell swallows my reflection.
You've become a current in the blue I drift on.
You've taught me to float like flotsam.
Is this the color of light?

Dawn squeezes a fresh lemon
over the horizon
and the boom cracks,
spinnakers fling half-moons
back to the wind
as the ocean spits.

O for a stable keel,
unflappable ballast,
white-lipped waves to kiss
the horizon with light. Where
a fish eagle may sculpt eyebrows
into the African sun, capture colours
that belong only to you.

I want to feed on migratory seabirds,
drink sweat beads between your breasts.

To drown beneath these waves,
leave behind their colours,
find new light
in an ultraviolet tsunami
with you.

CHRIS VAN DER WALT

The last autumn leaf

from the apple tree soared
without a care.
It came to rest
without a fuss
and rippled a wry smile
from the composure
of the coy pond:
shattering
its soft incarnate gaze.

And yet, there
yes, right there on the surface –
something else undulates
around the re-composited reflection:
it's unable to become visible,
it would like to stay alive
but has no idea how,
it turns away from your gaze,
still born, despite
a caesarian birth.

                    CHRIS VAN DER WALT

Far Away

This man is far away from his trees.

He squats above a concrete ground
legs gnarled in travel, talking of
rootlessness.

And yet, those legs are strong and
his words are strong. Rooted,

they journey back along
a road embraced by trees.

When he speaks of his far away trees
they tunnel around,

broken branches tumble into the room
until his eyes are falling leaves

shaded by love.

Voice forested,
head bowed, dark silver hair

curled like lichen
snow-kissed, around his bent neck,
the trees canopy him,

this far away man.

    TANIA VAN SCHALKWYK

Fathomless

There is a fathomless ocean
and it swallows
as it kisses.

In this sea, there are reefs with
edges that fall into steep holes.
You can sit on the coral

dangle your feet into the precipice

let your ankles be nibbled
watch the shades of blue blur,

listen to the man in the sea calling you to come to him –

and you could dive into his cold, hard arms
sink into the endless story of his dark eyes
drink in his salt,

lay down at the bottom of his bed –

or you could wait for a current to take you away,
pull you away from his embrace
pull you out further and further into the open –

floating out, in the deep
arms spread out to the sun,
hair skimming the surface

you may feel peace
may think you have let go
until you sense you are not alone –

the swish and splash of a fin,
the glint of a mouth hungry for you
the tug on your locks, pull on your limbs

recalls you to him, reminds you

of the descent, the day you will be devoured,
of the night you will surrender, the one time
you will stop treading, stop swimming

and allow yourself to drown, fathomless.

      TANIA VAN SCHALKWYK

Matchstick Girl

The sky fell from her eyes.
The city flew through her mouth.
The wind wept with her.

She tasted electricity
as she chased the moon
in a car at night, and the sun up a mountain the next day.

The light she wanted, the one she read about –
the light she saw promenading streets and perculating
    trees,
escaped her hands.

Instead she lit up,
as from within, a fluorescent city bulb,
burning everything she could write about – blocks of
    home, timber of lives.

TANIA VAN SCHALKWYK

Biographies

About the compiler

Liesl Jobson is a photographer, musician and writer. She is the author of *100 Papers*, which won the 2005 Ernst van Heerden Award; *View from an Escalator*, poetry; and a short story collection, *The Edge of the Pot*. She is a senior correspondent at Books LIVE and edits the South African domain of Poetry International. She is a single sculler and an ocean rower.

About the contributors

Ingrid Andersen's poetry has been published in local and international journals for over 18 years. She has two volumes of poetry: *Excision* (2004) and *Piece Work* (2010). Her influences include the French Romantic poets, Imagism and the writings of Hughes and Bashō. She is founding editor of *Incwadi*, an online South African journal that explores the interaction between poetry and image. She was born in Johannesburg, studied English literature (Wits) and is presently completing a Masters in adult education. An activist Anglican priest living in the KwaZulu-Natal Midlands, she works in human rights, healing and reconciliation.

Christine M Coates has loved poetry since childhood. Various literary journals have published her poems: *New Coin*, *New Contrast*, *Incwadi*, *Carapace*. In 2010 *Living with My X* was published by Random House Struik. She has written a family memoir and a novel as part of an MA

(Creative Writing) at UCT and is currently working on her third novel and a collection of poetry. She works as a writing coach, teaches creative writing and also enjoys making creative hand-made books. Christine lives in Cape Town.

Gail Dendy has published seven collections of poetry, her latest being *Closer Than That* (Dye Hard Press, 2011). She was first published in the UK by Harold Pinter, with subsequent collections appearing in South Africa, Britain and America. Her poetry appears in local and overseas anthologies, most recently in an anthology of Greville Press poems (Carcanet, UK, 2010) which includes works by Harold Pinter. Throughout the 1980s and early '90s Gail pioneered contemporary dance in South Africa and was nominated for the inaugural AA Vita Award for Best Performer. She is currently the information specialist for an international corporate-law firm.

Dawn Garisch has had five novels and a collection of poetry, *Difficult Gifts,* published, as well as a short play and short film produced. She has written for television and newspapers. Three of her novels have been published in the UK, and in 2010 *Trespass* was nominated for the Commonwealth prize in Africa. She won the DALRO prize for poetry in 2007. A work of non-fiction, *Eloquent Body*, will be published by Modjaji Books this year. She is a practising medical doctor and lives in Kalk Bay.

Anthea Garman is an associate professor teaching writing and editing and media studies in the School of Journalism and Media Studies at Rhodes University. Before becoming an academic she worked as a journalist for the *Rand Daily*

Mail, *Cape Times*, *Sunday Times* and *Natal Witness*. Her doctoral thesis is on Antjie Krog, South Africa's poet-public intellectual. She edits the *Rhodes Journalism Review*.

Denise Gray is a PhD student in English at Stellenbosch University. She heralds from Durban and nurtures a sentimental attachment to the sea. In her travels she has worked as a receptionist, a ballet teacher and a communications lecturer before deciding to pursue a career in academia. She jogs and meditates for her mental health, has a close but fraught relationship with the bible, and is most alive when she is with people. From her mother she has inherited an obsession with dust mites and a desperate attachment to the colour red.

Dorian Haarhoff is a poet, storyteller and mentor who runs creative writing and storytelling workshops. He uses storytelling, writing, images and symbolic work as a means of discovering hidden potential and assessing new ways of being and seeing. A former Professor of English (University of Namibia) he has also taught in a Canadian Creative Writing Faculty. Dorian has thrice been invited as a poet and as a guest storyteller to the Conference of Word Affairs in Boulder, Colorado. He has appeared at Poetry Africa, Durban, and at the International Poetry Festival in Colombia, South America. He lives in Somerset West.

Megan Hall won the Ingrid Jonker Prize for her debut collection of poetry, *Fourth Child* (Modjaji Books, 2007). She appeared at the Poetry Africa Festival in 2008 and at the Badilisha Poetry X-Change in 2009. Her work has appeared in local journals *New Contrast*, *New Coin*, *Fidelities*, and *Botsotso*; online at *Incwadi*, the Poetry

International website and *Big Bridge*; as well as in the *Worldscapes* and *Leaves to a Tree* anthologies (edited by Robin Malan). She lives in Cape Town with her family, and publishes dictionaries and school literature for Oxford University Press Southern Africa.

Geoffrey Haresnape is a poet and writer of fiction with four volumes of poetry published to date: *Drive of the Tide* (1976), *New-Born Images* (1991), *Mulberries in Autumn* (1996) and *The Living and the Dead: Selected and New Poems* (2005). His two prose fiction titles are *Testimony* (1991) and *African Tales from Shakespeare* (1999). His fifth volume of poetry, *Where the Wind Wills*, is due out shortly from Echoing Green Press. He is Emeritus Professor of English at the University of Cape Town.

Siddiq Khan lives in Cape Town, where he was born at 8 o'clock on a shrill April evening in the year 1990. A product of his times, his time's been spent within the murderously narrow range of passions, adventures, threats and opportunities presented to him by his society, of whom he is an irreconcilable enemy. His writing is both the result and the (all too partial) negation of this thoroughly dissatisfying situation.

Nosipho Kota was born in New Brighton, Port Elizabeth. She has been a feature writer for two regional newspapers. Her poetry has appeared in various journals and anthologies, including *Kotaz*, *Carapace*, *Fidelities* and *Nobody Ever Said Aids*. She has freelanced for the *Oprah Magazine*, *Madiba Action* and *Sunshine Coast Living*. In 2010 her first poetry collection, *Bare Soul*, was published through Swii Arts Amendment with funding from the Centre for the Book and was launched at the Cape Town Book Fair. She is mother to Khwezi, a son, and Maya, a daughter.

Born and raised in the small coastal town of Margate, **Luisa Lagerwall** jumped at the opportunity to study in the big city. Never quite outgrowing her childhood imagination, she dreamed of writing stories and completed her degree studies in English and Media Communications (Hons) cum laude at the University of KwaZulu-Natal. University provided her the opportunity not only to be mentored and inspired by distinguished South African authors, but also to explore the writing process and to produce the collection of poetry 'her city visions' from which these poems were taken. When not writing, Luisa enjoys reading and photography.

Jennifer Lovemore-Reed is a contemporary artist living in Cape Town. She works in a variety of media including photography, mixed media, performance art, installation and video installation. She has taken part in many exhibitions locally and abroad. In 2004 she exhibited in Paris while attending an artists residency at the Cité Internationale des Arts, as part of the Vuleka art prize, which she won in 2003. Writing has always been an integral part of her creative life. Lovemore-Reed has had poetry published previously, but it is the act of writing herself onto the page that is most valuable to her.

Risimati Mathonsi was born near Makhado, Limpopo. A former schoolteacher and journalist, he is presently the editor the *Maputaland Mirror* and the co-director of the Islamic Inter-Faith Research Institute based in Durban. His poetry and short stories have appeared in *Staffrider*,

The Bloody Horse and *Research in African Literature*. In 1979 he received the Kwanza Award following an invitation to the Writers Congress in West Berlin. He is widely travelled and loves Fela Kuti, Osibisa, Salif Keita and the mystic poetry of Rumi. He speaks Zulu, Ndebele, Tshivenda, Shona, English, Xitsonga, Afrikaans, Sepedi and Kiswahili. His work-in-progress explores medieval Trans-Limpopo trade interaction between the VaTsonga Swahili, and VhaVenda with the Omani Arabs and the Shirazi Persians.

Kea' Modimoeng was born in Mafikeng and is the author of *Maduo*, a collection of Setswana poetry published in 2008. Throughout his artistic life, Kea' has collaborated with many poets, growing a vibrant local poetry and Motswako hiphop scene. He attended the 2008 inaugural Pan African Literary Forum Writers' Conference in Ghana. Modimoeng has written for the *Sunday Times* and is currently involved in arts-driven corporate social responsibility initiatives through the Lentswe Arts Projects. He was recently appointed to the council of the Windybrow Theatre. His website is www.keamodimoeng.co.za.

Tsela Moloi started writing while he was in exile in Tanzania and Bulgaria from 1978 to 1991. He describes those years as tough times during which he longed for his family and was concerned about their wellbeing, while at the same time, being involved in the struggle for the liberation of all South Africans. When he returned to South Africa, he continued writing. He reflects on political topics and social issues like the HIV/Aids pandemic and the high rate of unemployment, especially among the youth. He is currently writing about the stalwarts of the struggle in Sesotho.

Jackie Mondi is a black South African woman, a writer, poet and Aids activist. She is fascinated by the power of the written word and strives to harness this power to change people's lives. Her writing has been published in *Face of the Spirit: Illuminating a century of essays by South African Women*, *So Much To Tell Vol. 2: an anthology of South African women writing*, *Agenda*, *The South African Labour Bulletin*, *Wrapped Magazine*, *Sunday Times*, *City Press* and she was quoted in the *2009 Budget Speech*. Jackie lives in Johannnesburg with her husband, Lumkile, and son, Vuyo.

Kobus Moolman teaches creative writing at the University of KwaZulu-Natal in Durban. He has published six collections of poetry: *Time like Stone* (awarded the 2001 Ingrid Jonker Prize), *Feet of the Sky*, *5 Poetry*, *Separating the Seas* (winner of the 2010 South African Literary Award for Poetry), *Anatomy* (winner of the 2008 DALRO Prize) and *Light and After*. His play, *Full Circle*, won the 2004 PANSA award, and was published in 2007. He has also published a collection of radio plays, *Blind Voices*. In 2010 he edited *Tilling the Hard Soil*, an anthology of poetry, prose and art by South African writers living with disabilities.

Dashen Naicker was born in Durban in 1986. As a slam poet he has performed at numerous art and music festivals, including Splashy Fen and the National Arts Festival. In 2006 he won the Life Check All Elements freestyle battle and placed second in the same category at the African Hip Hop Indaba. In 2010 he was one of the Durban Spotlight poets at Poetry Africa and the winner of the annual Poetry Africa SlamJam. His lyrical poems have been published in online and print journals, locally and abroad. He holds an

MA in Creative Writing from the University of KwaZulu-Natal.

Puleng Nkomo is a writer, language activist and composer of choral music. He is keenly interested in folk songs, classical music and opera. His literary output includes poetry, drama, radio serials, novels, translations, language manuals and study guides. He was born in 1958 at Bongweni Location, Randfontein to Sara, a professional nurse, and Paul, a minister in the Dutch Reformed Church. Puleng is an educator specialising in North Sotho, history, social sciences, and arts and culture. He has a BA (University of Limpopo), BA Hons (University of Pretoria), HED (University of Limpopo), and PTC (Mokopane College of Education).

Martha Pretoors was born in Keimoes in the Northern Cape where her love of reading and poetry began at an early age. She matriculated from Hoërskool Oranjezicht in 1994. She works as an administrative assistant at the Durbanville Children's Home but enjoys creative endeavours like knitting, crochet and making greeting cards as well as trying out new recipes in the kitchen. She enjoys escaping the daily grind at the gym.

Gillian Rennie teaches writing and editing in the School of Journalism and Media Studies at Rhodes University. Before that she worked for a long time in a variety of print media. She has edited *Cue*, the daily newspaper of the National Arts Festival, since 1999 and was a USC Annenberg/Getty Arts Journalism Fellow in 2010. Her profile of MaMbeki in *Fairlady* won a Mondi Award for profile writing. She believes polka dots have the power to deliver joy, that starlight is a health drink and – setting aside their disregard for semicolons – that cats know everything.

Beverly Rycroft was born Beverly Graven in the Eastern Cape. She is a graduate of UCT and Wits. A qualified teacher, she has written for both local and international magazines, and in 2000 was joint winner of the Femina/ Sensa Features competition. In 2007 she enrolled with Finuala Dowling's poetry workshops. Since then, her poems have appeared in *Carapace, New Coin, scrutiny2* and *New Contrast*. Her first poetry collection, *missing,* was published in 2010 by Modjaji Books. Beverly has three children and lives in Cape Town with her family.

Karin Schimke, previously a political writer at *The Star* and *Cape Times*, is a freelance journalist and columnist. Apart from her journalistic work, she has written two works of non-fiction, a children's story and several short stories. Her poetry has been widely published, and her first collection, *Bare & Breaking*, is forthcoming from Modjaji Books. She works as a writing tutor and mentor, and is the books editor for the *Cape Times*.

Mavis Smallberg was a teacher during the 1980s and, driven by the socio-political upheaval of the time, started writing poetry. She worked with diverse cultural collectives while participating in various solo and group poetry performances. She was a founder member of COSAW (Congress of South African Writers) in Cape Town, and the performance poetry collective, WEAVE (Women's Educational, Artistic Voice Expression). She was the language editor for the anthology, *Ink @ Boiling Point* in 2002. Her poems appear in many South African and international anthologies. Mavis Smallberg lives in Cape Town and works as a heritage practitioner.

Abu Bakr Solomons was born in Cape Town and has taught English for some 30 years. He is currently the principal of Spes Bona High School, Athlone. He completed studies in English, psychology and history at the University of Cape Town, University of Western Cape and UNISA. In 1992 he was awarded a fellowship to pursue research on the works of Bessie Head and Alex La Guma at Northwestern University in Chicago. In 1993 he was selected to participate in the Salzburg Seminar in Austria. His poems have been published in various journals and in a recent anthology published by Botsotso.

Bhekani Thabede was born in Pongola, KwaZulu-Natal in 1974. His love of writing started at Ekucabangeni High School in the mid-80s when he started writing *Izinkomo zamabheka*, which won the 1999 and 2000 Usiba Writers Guild Award for Novel and Essay. Other works soon followed. He joined the SADF where he spent more than ten years as an infantry instructor. In 2003 he established Khula Arts centre where he is developing youth in arts and culture, including writing. Bhekani is the co-author of two books, *Izingwazi zanamuhla* and *IsiZulu sethu esicebile*. He is married to Dollana Thabede who is also a writer and they are settled in Richards Bay.

After being raised in the East Cape, **Chris van der Walt** spread his wings to Cape Town and Johannesburg. He now lives in Port Elizabeth and has recently started writing.

Tania van Schalkwyk is the hybrid of a Hamburg sailor and a Mauritian artist, born in Africa, raised in Arabia and matured in Europe. She recently followed Cupid to Milan, where she is working on her second collection, centred around the themes of the stranger, the other, and the water as male muse. Creatively, Tania is exploring live collage, spontaneous sounding/singing and improvised skits in the shower, in collaboration with fellow play-fools, and anywhere brave enough to host her. She teaches English, Creative Writing and Creative Contact. Her first book, *Hyphen*, published by UCT Writers won the Ingrid Jonker Prize. Her website is www.alchemyofthebody.com.

What is the European Union?

The European Union is a unique economic and political partnership between 27 European countries* that has delivered half a century of peace, stability, and prosperity, helped raise living standards, launched a single European currency, and is progressively building a single Europe-wide market in which people, goods, services and capital move among Member States as freely as within a country.

Created in the aftermath of the Second World War, the first steps taken towards a union were to foster economic cooperation. Since then, the union has developed into a huge single market. What began as a purely economic union has evolved into an organisation spanning all areas, from development aid to environmental policy.

The EU actively promotes human rights and democracy and has the most ambitious emission reduction targets for fighting climate change in the world. Thanks to the abolition of border controls between EU countries, it is now possible for people to travel freely within most of the EU.

How does it work?

European Union countries have set up institutions to run the European Union and adopt its legislation. The main ones are:
- European Parliament (representing the people of Europe)
- Council of the European Union (representing national governments)
- European Commission (representing the common EU interest)

Size and population
At 4 million km² the European Union is roughly one seventh the size of Africa and just over three times the size of South Africa. France is the EU's largest country and Malta its smallest. The EU has a population of close to 500 million people – the world's third largest after China and India.

European Union symbols
- The European flag – the 12 stars in a circle symbolise the ideals of unity, solidarity and harmony among the peoples of Europe.
- The European anthem – the melody used to symbolise the EU comes from Ludwig Van Beethoven's 9th Symphony composed in 1823.
- Europe Day – the ideas behind the European Union were first put forward on 9 May 1950 by French foreign minister Robert Schuman. This is why 9 May is celebrated as a key date for the EU.
- The EU motto – "United in diversity"

The European Union and South Africa – a Partnership of Equals
The growing relationship between South Africa and the European Union since 1994 has been underpinned by the Trade, Development and Cooperation Agreement (TDCA). Closer ties between the two parties were consolidated in 2007 with the establishment of the EU–SA Strategic Partnership.

This partnership, the only one of its kind with an African partner, is centered on enhanced political dialogue around issues of shared interest including climate change, the global economy, governance, bilateral trade, and peace and security matters. In line with this, its action plan encompasses sectoral cooperation on a range of issues such as climate change, environment, education, science and technology, space, trade, migration, etc.

Annual summits and ministerial and senior officials' meetings steer the partnership along with the EU–South Africa Joint Cooperation Council. They provide the occasions to discuss current bilateral, regional and global issues.

Trade cooperation

The European Union remained South Africa's number one trading partner in 2010, accounting for 28% of the value of total SA trade flows. The EU is the most important destination for local exports, accounting for just over 23% of total exports from South Africa. Similarly, the EU remains the biggest source for SA imports at some 32% of total imports.

Development cooperation

The European Union is South Africa's most important development partner by far, providing close to 70% of all external assistance funds. The total indicative budget for the period 2007–13 amounts to € 980 million, the largest bilateral envelope worldwide. The EU, its Member States and the European Investment Bank (EIB) annually invest in South Africa over € 500 million in grants and loans.

More information can be found at http://eeas.europa.eu/south_africa/

---

* Belgium, Bulgaria, Czech Republic, Denmark, Germany, Estonia, Ireland, Greece, Spain, France, Italy, Cyprus, Latvia, Lithuania, Luxembourg, Hungary, Malta, the Netherlands, Austria, Poland, Portugal, Romania, Slovenia, Slovakia, Finland, Sweden, and the United Kingdom.